VOYAGEUR COUNTRY

The Fesler-Lampert *Minnesota Heritage Book* Series

This series is published with the generous assistance of the John K. and Elsie Lampert Fesler Fund and David R. and Elizabeth P. Fesler. Its mission is to republish significant out-of-print books that contribute to our understanding and appreciation of Minnesota and the Upper Midwest.

The Gift of the Deer by Helen Hoover

The Long-Shadowed Forest by Helen Hoover

Listening Point by Sigurd F. Olson

The Lonely Land by Sigurd F. Olson

Runes of the North by Sigurd F. Olson

The Singing Wilderness by Sigurd F. Olson

Voyageur Country: The Story of Minnesota's National Park by Robert Treuer

Voyageur Country

The Story of Minnesota's
National Park

Robert Treuer

University of Minnesota Press

MINNEAPOLIS

LONDON

First paperback printing, 1998

Financial assistance for the preparation of the manuscript for
this volume was provided by the Elmer L. and Eleanor J. Andersen
Foundation.

Published by the University of Minnesota Press
111 Third Avenue South, Suite 290
Minneapolis, MN 55401-2520
http://www.upress.umn.edu

A CIP record is available from the Library of Congress.

ISBN 0-8166-3155-7

Printed in the United States of America on acid-free paper

The University of Minnesota is an equal-opportunity
educator and employer.

10 09 08 07 06 05 04 03 02 01 00 99 98   10 9 8 7 6 5 4 3 2 1

*Dedicated to the Indians of the
Minnesota north country who have
lived there for thousands of years
without damaging it, and to the
voyageurs of the fur trade who
respected and loved this land
and the people living there.*

CONTENTS

PREFACE TO THE PAPERBACK EDITION

This book explores the long and complex origins, history, development, and role of Voyageurs National Park. Minnesota's only national park abuts the Canadian border and is a place notable for its granite grandeur and four large lakes. Adjoining it to the east is the Quetico-Superior wilderness, a maze of interconnecting lakes and rivers encompassing Quetico Provincial Park in Ontario and the Boundary Waters Canoe Area Wilderness (BWCAW) in the Superior National Forest. So spectacular is the wild beauty of this region that efforts to safeguard it date from the nineteenth century, prior to widespread logging of the area, and have attracted a national constituency.

We inhabit a planet with many sites that elicit wonder and admiration at the manifold beauties of creation and humanity's links with it, yet this particular patch of planet is one of a kind. Its origins, geology, archaeology, history, ecology, and politics are unique and exciting. Forests, rivers, lakes, and the massive granite of the Precambrian shield, Earth's oldest exposed mantle, combine into a vast area of beauty that has touched the hearts and spirits of many. Despite forbidding climate it has drawn and challenged flora, fauna, and people since time immemorial; increasing evidence suggests human habitation long before the last ice age. So awesome are the cliffs, forests, and waters that they have been as a magnet to spirituality and aesthetics for millennia.

The first whites in the area discovered what Native Americans had known long before—that this wild beauty somehow touched the human soul. French missionaries and fur traders said so, as did all who followed. Decades before logging began in the area in the 1880s, Christopher Andrews, Civil War veteran, forester, and founder of

Minnesota's fire warden system, urged preserving and protecting it. In the twentieth century, Sigurd Olson, Ernest Oberholtzer, Florence and Lee Jaques, Arnold Bolz, and many others have written about, painted, and photographed it. Local residents cope with the coldest temperatures in the continental United States because, as some say, "It's the most beautiful place on Earth." Living—sometimes even visiting—there challenges human fortitude and rewards with a sense of wonder and gratitude at the splendor.

This wonderland has not always been treated well by people during the past three hundred years. The fur trade commercially exploited fauna and inhabitants until its collapse in 1848. Native Americans, weaned from hunting/gathering to dependence on manufactured goods, were abandoned, and subsequent starvation and disease killed an estimated two-thirds of the native population in the next half century. Principal large game, notably woodland caribou and elk, was hunted to extinction to feed the logging and railroad camps; wolves were also hunted and poisoned to near extinction. Mature climax forests were wiped out and intense fires of remaining slash interfered with natural regeneration and damaged the thin mantle of soil overlaying the granite. Food chains were disrupted and destroyed, and ecosystem processes were altered. Yet beauty survived these onslaughts to the point where growing numbers of people have strived to preserve and protect it while others want to use and exploit it. This debate set the stage for the struggle and conflict out of which Voyageurs National Park came into being in 1970.

Lake Superior is to the east, the now-exhausted Mesabi Iron Range to the south, boreal forest and tundra to the north. To the southwest is the nation's first national forest, the Chippewa. Several Canadian Indian Reserves are to the north. United States Reservations in the region are Leech Lake, White Earth, Bois Forte (Nett Lake), Fond du Lac (about twenty miles upstream from Duluth on the St. Louis River), and historic and spectacularly beautiful Grand Portage on Lake Superior at the Canadian border. The human scale encompasses prehistoric inhabitants in a long succession of tribes and cultures who wished the freedom to live according to their beliefs of how humans should relate to creation. Then came fur traders, missionaries, and logging and railroad barons, who eventually collided with those who wished to protect, preserve, and if possible regenerate a viable ecosystem in a framework of surviving beauty as a national treasure for the benefit of the current and future public.

North of a line from Duluth to Warroad the land is sparsely populated and over 70 percent of it is public domain—state forests and parks, tax-forfeited acreages, game preserves, and federal lands. This is a consequence not only of remoteness and climate but also of economic disasters: collapse of the fur trade, logging off of the big timber, exhaustion of the iron ore mines, and failure of commercial fishing, among others. Small communities; logging, wood, and paper companies; resorts and collateral services; Indian Reservations; and a dwindling number of smallhold farms dot the remainder of this land.

In the 1950s the renewed proposal to establish a national park in this region regained momentum. To Minnesota's governor during the early 1960s, Elmer L. Andersen, such a proposal made economic and environmental sense, matched by taconite development to revive the devastated iron range. The proposal was sparked by the Voyageurs National Park Association (VNPA, later renamed Voyageurs Region National Park Association), a private nonprofit organization. Many notables, including Sigurd Olson, Ernest Oberholtzer, Aldo Leopold, Rep. John Blatnik, and Charles Lindbergh, espoused the proposal. Local, state, and ultimately national support developed and was lobbied vigorously in Washington.

Congress passed the Voyageurs National Park bill in 1970 and President Richard Nixon signed it in 1971. The State of Minnesota then had to transfer its forestland holdings within the designated park boundaries to the United States. At the instigation of State Representative Irv Anderson (whose International Falls district included portions of the park), the state land transfer legislation also provided for the creation of a tax-funded Citizens Council on Voyageurs National Park, which in essence duplicated the already existing and privately funded VNPA. The council's function was to provide local and citizen input on park policies and management. It continues in existence, as does its tax-supported funding, under the tight personal control of Anderson.

Not long after Voyageurs Park was formally established, the Citizens Council succeeded in obtaining a revision of the boundaries, opening a portion of Black Bay to duck hunting. This early success triggered subsequent demands foreign to U.S. national parks. The

Citizens Council became a lightning rod and catalyst for national organizations opposed to public land management and enforceable environmental protection.

An adroit politician, Anderson, who still holds office, has used the Citizens Council to stir election-year issues appealing to sportsmen, users of mechanized vehicles, and northwoods folks delighted to thumb their noses at their wealthier metropolitan cousins. In the political climate of the 1980s and 1990s, the fledgling Voyageurs National Park has been under repeated siege. There were demands from the Citizens Council that the only national park in the Land of 10,000 Lakes admit jet skis, snowmobiles, pontoon boats, and fly-in planes on its four lakes, and that snowmobile trails be created in the park in addition to the several thousand miles of such tax-supported trails already in existence in the state, some in the vicinity. The council opposes wilderness designation for the Kabetogama Peninsula, which is entirely within the park boundaries, home to timber wolves and moose, and was once considered a potential location for reintroducing woodland caribou.

During the 1996 political season the rhetoric about Voyageurs National Park and the Boundary Waters Canoe Area Wilderness once again became mercilessly strident. Minnesota Senator Paul Wellstone was up for reelection and striving to be a peacemaker. He brought in the Federal Mediation and Conciliation Service to facilitate a compromise. This put the Senator above the fray, but it put a national interest and mandate on a par with local, vested, and political interests. As has happened elsewhere, once a national park is established, local enterprises on the periphery flourish and grow, and the economy prospers. Around Voyageurs Park resorts were upgraded and improved, tourist trade increased, and the money flow into the area continues upward, much as Gov. Elmer L. Andersen predicted long ago. However, the election-year rhetoric, cutting across party lines, remains.

The federal mediators set up panels for Voyageurs and for BWCAW to deal with the separate issues being raised. Public hearings were held, followed by meetings with representatives of environmental groups, interested persons, the statewide VRNPA, the Citizens Council, park officials, resort operators, and snowmobile club officers. The BWCAW panel deadlocked mainly on the issue of four truck portages and failed to come up with a resolution. The Voyageurs Park panel worked out a labored compromise.

Jet skis and fly-in planes were out, rental pontoon boats would receive an agreed-upon number of permits (giving park officials some control over the dumping of trash), and some snowmobile trails would be created (desirable in areas where lake ice was at times undermined and weakened by currents). A document emerged and appeared to have the approval of all participants. After the election the agreement was repudiated by Anderson's Citizens Council and a snowmobile organization, throwing the mediation effort into limbo.

No one patch of Earth can meet all demands of a growing human population and dwindling wildlife and natural resources. Even where we seek to control impact and restrict use, as in BWCAW campsites, the land must be retired for several years after a few years of use. We love the land to death at best, and exploit it to sterility at worst.

The United States invented and pioneered the national park concept, emulated worldwide. We are now testing the European role model of the regional park in the New York Adirondacks and the New Jersey Pine Barrens. A regional park, or greenlined area, includes publicly owned, private, commercial, and industrial lands, and inhabitants. It protects and safeguards current ownership and activities, cultures, and traditions. It is zoned and governed by a body composed of private interests and federal, state, and local governments. A geographic entity's remaining beauties, peoples, and cultures are both protected and preserved.

The advantages to regional parks are many. No land needs to be purchased, because all land within a greenlined regional park—private, commercial, industrial, state, federal—is covered by a zoning code administered by a board, which includes all governmental units and affected interests.

Another advantage is that present residents and enterprises are safeguarded, and that the character and cultures can continue assured that future changes will not destroy or diminish them or the quality of the land, which is the source of their livelihoods and of the quality of their chosen lives. Multiple cultures, cooperatives, arts, and crafts can be encouraged. The land itself will not be further denigrated or its remaining wildlife further jeopardized; instead, opportunities are created to nurture endangered species and introduce some that have been wiped out. The unique beauty within the boundaries of

Voyageurs National Park and the BWCAW would be safe, if not safer, under this regional park concept, as would be the lives of the present inhabitants so eager to preserve the quality of what they have and prize yet also needing to be able to make a living.

Failure of the 1996 federal mediation effort proves that all wishes and desires cannot be crowded into the small canvas of Voyageurs National Park, though they should be heeded. The greenlined or regional park concept may prove to be a way to respect all interests and accommodate them in balance in a sufficiently large area. One patch of land cannot accommodate it all; a larger one, if planned and zoned, might.

Other proposed national parks are waiting in the wings, each with its proponents and detractors, its unique attributes, histories, and problems. There has long been talk of a tall-grass prairie national park. A study of demographics by Princeton geographers published in 1992 led to the dismaying realization that the population was disappearing in county after county on the high western plains as a consequence of dropping groundwater tables, with many counties virtually depopulated. This change led to consideration of establishing a "buffalo commons" for some of this area, a controversial and hotly debated idea but potentially the core of a new national park. Vast stretches of federally owned grasslands leased at a pittance, a subsidy, some say, to cattle corporations, are exhausted and increasingly subject to erosion, their days numbered and their lands possible candidates for preservation. The high plains of America's midlands offer an object lesson in what can happen when we do not heed what we are doing to the land: ultimately it may no longer be able to sustain the people or itself. The people leave and the land lies fallow.

Whatever the needs and desires of future generations to preserve and protect the land so that the people might flourish aesthetically and economically, Voyageurs National Park serves as a bellwether for the future. The unfolding story of Voyageurs will forecast our nation's valuing of the land that hosts and nurtures us.

ACKNOWLEDGMENTS

I am indebted to the historical research and publications of R. Newell Searle, particularly his work *Saving Quetico-Superior: A Land Set Apart*, published by the Minnesota Historical Society in 1977, and his article on the creation of the Chippewa National Forest, "The Politics of Compromise," *Minnesota History*, fall 1971.

The staff, facilities, and resources of the Minnesota Historical Society and of the Koochiching County Historical Society were most helpful. It is a pleasure to work with people who are both competent and cooperative. The National Park Service in Washington, at the Omaha Regional Office, and most of all at the International Falls headquarters of Voyageurs Park was forthcoming with information.

After meeting some of the many people involved in the effort to establish Voyageurs National Park, I gradually realized that not only did they bring about a successful change for the better but their participation in the process changed them. Martin Kellogg, a Minneapolis businessman who has worked steadfastly for the park since he helped found the Voyageurs National Park Association in 1963, pointed this out to me. "I wonder if there weren't character changes as we worked for the park," Kellogg said, "if we didn't change our views and values from one of tourist attraction to the need for conservation. It was so for me, and I think for Gov. Elmer Andersen and others as well."

Elmer Andersen, while governor of Minnesota and for many years as a private citizen, breathed life into the concept of the park and brought skill and insight to the campaign that consumed over ten years. At times it looked hopeless, yet every person I interviewed in the course of gathering material for this book credited Andersen, who had the respect of politicians from both parties, with bringing about the establishment of Voyageurs National Park.

Martin Kellogg spent many hours providing information for this book and contacting others who could assist me. Among them are U. W. Hella, Erick Kendall, Rita Shemesh, Lloyd Brandt, and Lon A. Garrison, who was with the Park Service when Voyageurs was proposed by Andersen. Myrl Brooks and Frank Ackerman at the park answered my importuning requests for information and vetted the manuscript, and Mary Lou Pearson dug out historical studies. At the University of Minnesota in Duluth, Dr. Richard W. Ojakangas, head of the Geology Department, had the thankless task of reading what a layman had written about his field of expertise. All errors are mine, not theirs—they tried to have me see the paths of righteousness.

Some people, briefly met, make a profound impression. It was so with earthy George Esslinger at International Falls; Ingvald Stevens, living alone but not lonely on his island in the park; and two former Park Service directors, George Hartzog and Conrad Wirth, whose dedication and knowledge were inspiring. Hartzog spoke about a Great Waterways proposal he and Interior Secretary Stewart Udall had sponsored for the Potomac River some years before. The region as a whole would be environmentally planned and would encompass parks, forests, game preserves, and recreation areas, as well as commercial and industrial enclaves. The concept was ahead of the times when proposed. It may yet be tested, perhaps between Grand Portage and Lake of the Woods.

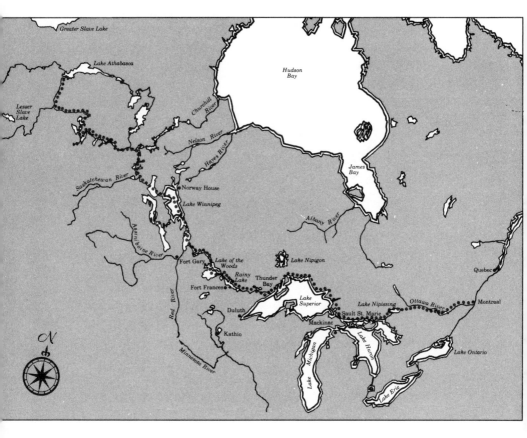

Voyageur country of North America, showing voyageurs' routes

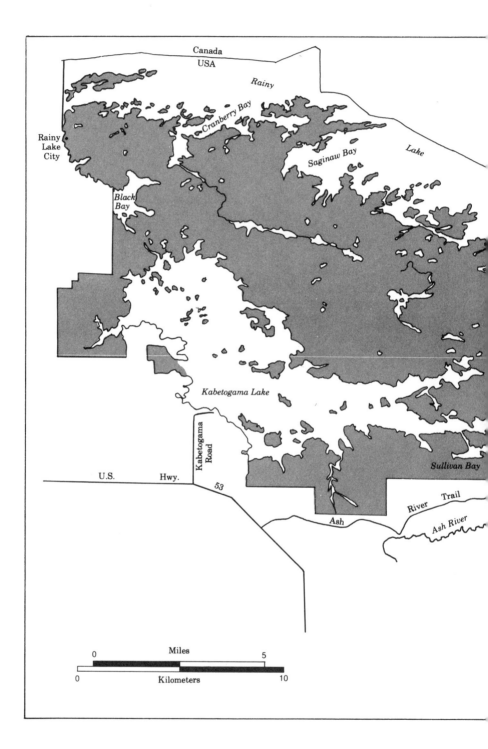

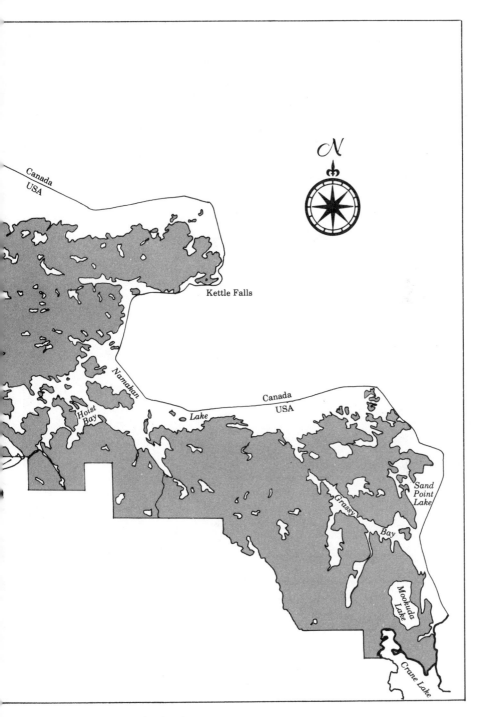

Voyageurs National Park

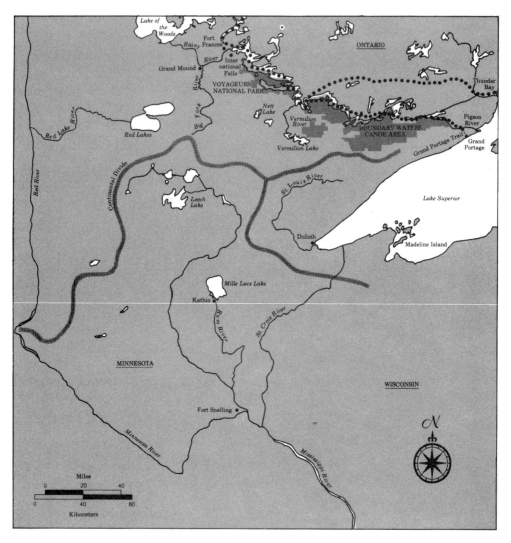

Voyageur trails along the Minnesota-Ontario border

VOYAGEUR COUNTRY

A Day's Cross-Country Skiing in Voyageurs Park

W*e each had our own motives and agendas. People usually do.*

At the sporting-goods store in International Falls where I rented cross-country skis and boots the night before, the owner chatted with me after sharpening a youngster's hockey skates and advising another on different ski waxes, some for cold weather, others for warmer days.

"I used to work for Boise Cascade," he said. "They wanted me to transfer to the main office in Idaho, and I couldn't bear to leave this country."

"The price of success?"

"I suppose. But it's hard to make a living here. I finally qualified and got a teacher's certificate, and am teaching school. My wife and I run this store, which I just love. You can say we stayed here because of the park. You going to ski in the park?"

"Tomorrow we'll drive to Ash River, ski up to Hoist Bay and around some of the Namakan Islands."

Prologue

"It should be a good day for it."

It was the end of winter. There were still over two feet of snow on the thick lake ice. Melting and the breakup of the ice was still wishful thinking, but the fish houses were being dragged from the ice on the off chance that it would warm up any day.

"I've canoed through the border lakes and in the Quetico," I told him, "but this is my first winter visit here." I expounded on my private theory that short, bowlegged people such as I have an advantage over tall, longlegged folks on snowshoes. I had tramped over a proposed loop trail on the Kabetogama Peninsula of Voyageurs National Park that day with naturalist Frank Ackerman, who wanted to show me the difference between logged areas in the roadless, rocky terrain and some spots where bigger timber remained. Padding over the deep snow was a lovely way to get around, quiet and easy, like scuffing over the surface of life without disturbing what was underfoot. Until we came to deadfalls and thick tangles of brush. I had been confident about the expedition, having spent some time on snowshoes as a northerner, but a day-long cross-country-skiing expedition would be a different experience; I'd never tried the new equipment.

"You'll enjoy it," he said. "There are places out there you can't get to except on skis or snowshoes. Probably won't see another person all day, once you get into the park."

I looked dubiously at the skinny cross-country skis, so narrow compared to my old pair of wood downhill skis. Now, how would I manage on these? I'd willingly go anywhere, match skill with anyone on snowshoes or in a canoe, but I had little confidence about the morrow.

"These things are quite in demand now," the hardware-store man assured me. "We've got people coming up here all winter long to go cross-country skiing. It's like they said, the park is drawing more people all the time. I'm switching to those skis over there next year." They were even narrower.

As I left the friendly store I wondered about the attraction of the north country. Here was a competent engineer who preferred to change occupations, taking a teaching job at much less pay rather than move away and transfer to a better position, just to stay near the northwoods. And it was not merely a matter of toler-

4

*ating the long winter in order to enjoy the brief, brilliant temper-
ate times. I shared this madness and could not explain it either,
though my home was a hundred miles away in the rolling hill
country of the Minnesota north, not on the stark, dramatic granite
of the border lakes.*

*The morning dawned with a faint promise of sunshine amid un-
certain temperatures. Maybe fifteen above? Twenty? It was a bit
humid, making the cold penetrate clothes. Five of us gathered at
the park's administrative offices just outside International Falls,
longing for a bit more sleep and warmth but not admitting it. The
park building was a modest, one-story wood structure, temporary
housing until the permanent building could be erected a few miles
away on Black Bay of Rainy Lake. Frank Ackerman tried bustling
around and being efficient, gathering equipment, maps, and canteens, with indifferent success. Mary Lou Pearson, the International Falls schoolteacher who doubles as park historian, kept looking
longingly at the warm building when she thought no one was
watching. Bob Schultz, park ranger, just looked grim and sleepy,
drawn into himself. Clayton Cabeen, who had been transferred to
Voyageurs as its new administrative officer only three days before,
and had joined us at the last minute on the spur of the moment to
get his first look at the place, was excited and full of questions.*

*"Will I be warm enough in these clothes? How much water
should I take? Will we be gone all day?"*

*The hour-long drive from headquarters east to Ash River skirted
the park boundaries through bare, snowcapped fields on what was
once pine forest rooted in the glacial moraine. It had been home-
steaded after the logging, but farming was poor and most people
had found jobs in International Falls or in the woods for their primary income. Half the distance to Ash River the road crossed the
first granite ridge, and patches of spruce forest nudged toward the
highway.*

*"Look at that mess!" I complained about highway construction
that was broadening the two lanes to four. "That's the place where
we picked blueberries last year!" I knew that the berries would
come back after the turmoil of the work was done, and that the
highway would accommodate the growing number of park visitors
as well as local traffic, but I did not feel like being wise and gra-*

cious about the disruption. Deer were feeding among fallen trees and slashed branches by the wayside, looking to be in remarkably good condition for this late in winter. Ordinarily deer are scrawny and worn just before spring and the brushes and grasses green.

"That's easy food for them," Mary Lou commented. "Succulent." Her lovely Slovenian face had a drawn, worried look, and it seemed she was searching to find something good in the day. Anxious about keeping up once we began skiing? If so, she wasn't the only one.

"Yeah, those deer look good," Bob agreed. "But the herd may get smaller as the forests get older." Logging, fires, and brush, which follows both, provide feed for them.

"Wolf would then decline too," Frank said. "With fewer deer that happens. And the wolves don't pay attention to the Canadian border; trapping is allowed over there."

I had assumed that the Canadians were far ahead of us in wildlife conservation and protection of the environment, but in recent years I have learned this is not so. What I had taken as enlightened conservation policies were more the result of sparse population than of being forward looking. The Canadians had shown little inclination to cooperate by controlling pollutant emissions in the new Atikokan power plant nearby, or in matching American parklands across the border after setting aside the original Quetico Provincial Park in 1909.

We passed the turnoff to Kabetogama Lake, four or five miles away and out of sight. Last summer we had canoed there, putting out from the Wooden Frog State Campground, a rocky hill jutting into the clean, island-studded lake. Very old Norway pine towered over our tent, and a sheltered bay afforded fine swimming. Now the lake was covered with several feet of ice, that in turn layered by about two feet of wind-compacted snow. The only sounds among the big trees would be a few chickadees and nuthatches, small gusts of wind whistling from the northwest, and the occasional booming and echoing of the lake ice as it contracted and expanded in preparation for the changing season. Last summer we had an unwanted concert from the blaring car radio of a group of swimmers drowning out the calling of the loons on the lake. The radio did not diminish the beauty of the place, only our enjoyment of it.

The Ash River turnoff, inauspicious as country roads go, took me into an area I had not visited before. As a very young girl, my wife had come here with her family to pick blueberries. Hers is an Ojibway Indian family, and during lean years at her home on Leech Lake Reservation, about a hundred miles south, they came here to camp and berry. Local stores and resorts bought the fresh blueberries by the quart. The picking was hot work, and the youngsters were expected to keep at it all day, and to carry the backpack crates several miles from the berry patches along an old railroad grade to the parked car.

"It was so hot, and we were so tired, that when we saw one of those cold, clear springs along the embankment, we'd jump in with our clothes on," she once told me. "By the time we'd come to the next spring, we'd be dry and hot again." On one such hike she and some young cousins fired their slingshots into the woods. A pebble hit a bear they did not know was there, and the angry animal came charging out of the brush seeming bigger than life to the frightened children, who took off at a run.

"I dropped my slingshot!" The cousin panted.

"Go back and get it if you want it so much," another yelled. "You're the one who hit the bear."

"I didn't mean to. I didn't know he was there."

They reached the car, and their parents, without having stopped for a cooling dip. The bear had given up the chase somewhere along the line — they had not bothered to look back. My wife didn't remember how much of the day's harvest had been spilled on the way, but she recalled that she still had the packing crate on her back. "I wouldn't have dared come without it," she said. "They would have sent me back for it."

Long ago her uncles and other forebears had found logging jobs hereabouts. Before then some of her ancestors had lived here, trapping, hunting, harvesting berries in summer, wild rice in autumn, maple sugar in spring, as the Ojibway displaced the Crees and drove out the Sioux two hundred years ago and more.

The Ash River Trail curved and dipped, following the contours of the land over granite hills, along riverside marsh, leading toward Namakan Lake. When the big loggers came into this area less than a hundred years ago, and most of them only fifty or sixty years ago, they followed the valley for the best access across the rough terrain. Mary Lou had been researching the local history and found 43 logging-camp locations within the park and pictures of the temporary railroad built to haul the pine from the lake to the sawmills farther to the south and east.

The road crowded near the frozen river, then led to a small cluster of buildings and cabins, several hanging over the edge of the steep riverbank.

"These are the resorts?" I asked Frank, not believing that the sad, careworn structures were the ones that had been gerrymandered out of the park boundaries on the grounds that visitors would benefit from nearby facilities, and that the resorts would benefit from the visitors.

Frank said: "Most of them are not winterized, so they have a very short tourist season in the summer. It's a marginal business. Not enough to build up capital, which is what you need to offer modern, year-round lodgings."

It was full of ironies. If the resorters could modernize, there would be plenty of business now. Without the business, they could not hope to get the money. So there the structures sat, squat, ugly, and melancholy. Compounding the ironies, a number of resort owners just outside the park boundaries have been privately approaching park officials, offering to sell their holdings.

"Why doesn't the park buy them?" I asked Frank.

"We can't. They are outside the boundaries set by the legislation. There would have to be action by Congress before we could do that."

High hopes and expectations had gone into the exclusion of the Ash River, Kabetogama, and Crane Lake resorts from the park. Like others, I had thought this was sound public land policy. Now, face to face with the tawdriness of it, I was no longer sure. Perhaps over the years . . . with small business loans . . . Or some larger concern might buy them out, but then it could lead to another case of Muzak piped out over the wilderness. Would local zoning keep the activities of large concessionaires within reason, within ecological bounds?

We stopped along a row of mailboxes set cheek by jowl.

"We'll pick up Ingvald Stevens's mail, in case we get that far," Frank said blandly, though I caught quick, furtive glances between him, Mary Lou, and Bob. They casually explained that Mr. Stevens was an old-timer, one of two living within the park the year around. As private holdings were being purchased by the Park Service, owners had the option of staying on in their homes or leaving. Most left, but 92-year-old Mr. Stevens chose to live out his years in the cabin on an island in Namakan Lake, skiing four miles one way to get his mail, chopping his firewood.

"He's a wonderful old man," Mary Lou said, "I've been interviewing him for his recollections. It's part of our oral-history program."

We packed our lunches and canteens and put on our skis. I wore heavy corduroy knickers and thick wool kneesocks, the others wool pants, though Bob was lacing on some bilious green nylon puttees that slipped over the top of his boots and over his pants legs. I thought they looked old-fashioned and blinked at the iridescent green. We headed down the riverbank to follow Ash River out into the park.

Used to downhill skis, I braced myself for a quick slide down and a turn at the bottom. But the slide was slow and at the bottom the skis refused to turn. I'd have to learn an entirely new technique this day.

We plodded along in single file. Tiny streaks of snow meandered over the bindings of the skis, across my shoes, and I no longer thought of Bob's puttees as anachronistic footwear: they would keep the snow out of his shoes and feet, mine would be wet before long! I considered offering to trade one of my sandwiches for the use of the puttees, or maybe just one of them, but decided against it.

With a hellish roar two snowmobiles caught up with us, circled us wildly on the river ice like frantic dogs chasing their tails, lunged up the embankment and down again, and disappeared amid gas and oil fumes and a decibel level approaching sonic boom.

Prologue

"We'll be away from them in a few minutes," Frank reassured me. "They'll be out on the lake ice, and we'll be going overland to Hoist Bay along the railroad grade."

Frank thinks that snowmobile manufacturers, by catering to power and speed, are sacrificing durability and dependability, and also pricing the vehicles out of the market. There once were over a hundred snowmobile manufacturers, and now about half a dozen are left, while inventories of unsold units continue to grow. For some people in the north country, snowmobiles are means of livelihood, transportation, and survival. It seems a pity their manufacture and use have been diverted into a craze for speed, and that planned obsolescence prevents people on low incomes, who could have practical use for them, from buying and maintaining them.

Up on the old railroad embankment I wondered whether this was the one my wife had hiked as a berry-picking youngster. Hot weather seemed light years away in the damp cold, and the wind had become more blustery, scudding grey clouds above our heads. Below our trail the rusted tops of ancient cars, deserted here many years ago, protruded through the ice and snow. Frank, Bob, and summer-student helpers have been clearing such debris, but some remains to be dragged out and hauled away. It amazes me that people can so wantonly despoil a place of beauty. No wonder we have to have parks, with regulations and rangers, paid for with our taxes, if we want some beauty left. Incredible.

There were some good-sized Norway pine here and there, little trees when logging was over, but formidable now at a hundred years and older. Mixed in were spruce, birch, poplar or aspen, tag alder, and occasionally cedar, balsam, and white pine. We had gone less than three miles when the brush crowded in over the embankment and we had to break trail to make headway.

We took turns breaking branches with our hands, shoving deadfalls out of the way. It was very slow going, and I wished for my trusty old snowshoes left behind in the car, or a short-handled ax. Better yet, both. We stopped to rest and consult the map. It was past noon, we were nowhere near the lake yet. Should we turn back? Why were they asking me? I hadn't been here before and had no concept of how far we had to go once we came out on Namakan, and I said so.

Prologue

"I haven't been here either," Frank confessed. He and Bob had often talked about this old railroad grade as a potential cross-country ski trail, and my visit was an opportunity to look it over. "We'll brush it out next summer," he promised. "Now that I've seen how overgrown it is."

I was reluctant to turn back before reaching the best part of the trip.

"We've only got another mile of this at most," I pleaded. "If we come out on the lake in an hour, we ought to be able to make the loop around to the next bay and go back up Ash River from there.

"All right," Frank agreed. "And if it gets too late, we can skip going all the way around past Stevens's place, and take the mail back to the mailbox."

Mary Lou still looked worried; she had kept up through the brush, though once or twice she had fallen, as had each of us. The snow was too deep to do without the skis, and the brush too thick for easy progress. Bob and I were breaking trail, certain we were nearing the lake, when Mary Lou fell again, and this time had to take a considerable rest before continuing.

"Maybe we ought to take the shortest way back," I suggested.

"She really wants to go on," Frank said. "Let's see how it goes."

The brush thinned, and on an open stretch of grade beginning the downhill slope to the lake we crossed otter tracks in the snow. Then we were in a clearing among resort cabins now used by the Park Service as a summer work camp. We took another look at the map. Stevens's cabin was still several miles away. If we omitted the side trip to his place, we would get back to our cars by late afternoon. If we went all the way, it would be dusk or later. It seemed unneighborly to me not to visit the old man living by himself and do him the courtesy of dropping off his accumulated mail. But I was also concerned about Mary Lou, who did not look at all well.

"If we take the short loop, we'll be turning left about a mile and a half up the bay," I said. "We've got to go that way anyhow, it will be faster than going back through the brush. Maybe two of us can go all the way to Stevens's, and the other two can take Mary Lou back to the car."

We ate quickly in the shelter of one of the buildings, our skis stuck in the deep snow while we stamped our feet and tried not to

11

let on that we were cold. Then we followed the slope of the land down to the lake ice, over the frost heaves of the ice, and out onto Namakan Lake. Trestle timbers weathering and rotting dotted out into the lake, protruding above the ice in uneven, serried patterns, and then stopped. This was where the logging railroad had ended, scooping up the great pines from the log booms. The shoreline was granite topped by new forest, the dramatic, beautiful north country looking as it did when the voyageurs were here, and the fur traders, and my wife's ancestors.

The narrow skis slipped, scudded over the uneven snow, occasionally pressing down an inch or two where the wind was whipping flakes into tiny dunes. I was becoming used to the feel of the skis, getting some slide and rhythm. We passed the turnoff to Moose Bay, which was the shortcut back, and everyone went on, Mary Lou deciding that even if she brought up the rear, she would come nevertheless. A mile, another, then around the headland with clusters of granite islands—I caught a faint whiff of smoke in the numbing wind.

"He's burning popple," I said. Frank grinned broadly. We could not see the cabin yet. Then the log outbuildings came into view, soon after the cabin with windblown white smoke coming from the chimney.

We tramped up the path to the house, saw the old man through the window as he sat at a desk, writing. He did not see or hear us, and we had to knock hard several times before he came to let us in.

"I didn't expect you anymore!" he said. "It got so late. . . . I called into town, and they said you were coming, but when it got so late . . ." There were tears in his eyes. Old age? Emotion? He was a thin, ramrod-backed man with white hair and bright blue eyes. There was stubble on his face and he looked emaciated, sallow. I didn't know he'd been expecting us.

Mary Lou hugged him, looked at him closely, hugged him again.
"Are you all right?" she asked.

"Better. I've been sick three days, couldn't hold down any food. I couldn't stand up or walk, I had to crawl out to the shed to get firewood. That's why I called. I thought I had a heart attack. But I'm all right now, just weak."

She obviously cared deeply about Ingvald Stevens. It went far beyond obtaining interesting interviews for the oral-history collection. The proud, self-sufficient recluse who declined all offers of assistance had been helpless and telephoned her, and that was why she had come, pushing herself beyond fatigue, afraid we might be too late. Even when he was very ill and uncomfortable, Mr. Stevens had not accepted the suggestion that a resort operator be sent out on a snowmobile to check on him. But if Mary Lou could come . . .

"I was so relieved when we smelled the smoke," Frank told me on the way back in. "That's when I knew he was still alive. I expected to find him dead."

"Why didn't you tell me?" I asked.

"We didn't know if we could get all the way to his place, and we didn't want to worry you."

We hauled firewood, did chores, and made sure he was able to care for himself. A snowmobile was sent from an Ash River resort to bring Mary Lou back in. The rest of us skied. It was sunset as we plodded over the lake, getting colder and windier, and I pulled the ski goggles out of my jacket pocket to shield my eyes from the sandy, driven snow grains blowing almost horizontally across the ice. The sunset colors filtering through the clouds tinted the landscape and some of the overcast mauve, light gold, and beige.

As we had left Ingvald Stevens I thought the winter must seem long to him. It does to all of us, despite our year-round love of the north. Even a self-reliant, self-disciplined man who has chosen to live by himself, maintaining a meticulous notebook and diaries, and going on skis for his mail, must relish the coming of yet another spring. So at the door I had said: "I saw a bald eagle today. They're back. He was sitting in a treetop. Very close."

Back in the protection of the park.

"A bald eagle! That's good! It'll be spring soon when the bald eagles return," Ingvald Stevens had said, his eyes no longer watery, but bright and smiling as he saw us off.

1

Wilderness Trail through Time

When the border between the United States and what is now Canada was being established after the War of 1812 and agreement was reached that it should follow the Great Lakes on the east and the 49th Parallel on the west, the 300-mile stretch from Lake Superior to Lake of the Woods posed a problem. It was a funnel of sorts, a granite kingdom of stark beauty and hazards with an ancient heritage and history no one then suspected. There was deep forest and a web of interconnecting lakes and rivers. Gorges, waterfalls, and rapids forced travelers to debark, carry canoe and contents around the obstacle, and resume travel after a portage. Winter travel was particularly hazardous and difficult in the harsh climate.

Both Britons and Americans wanted the Mississippi River headwaters on *their* side of the border, and they suspected that this potential trade route started somewhere "up there." Negotiators did not know where and the treaty talks bogged down. On paper,

France, Spain, England, and the United States had, in turn, claimed sovereignty over this remote land. Among the Europeans only the French fur traders knew it well, and they were not parties to the treaty talks, having lost Canada to the British in 1763. The prolonged jockeying ended in 1842 after it had become clear that no amount of finagling could place the source of the Mississippi on the British side of the line. (In 1832 Indians guided Henry Schoolcraft to it in west-central Minnesota, more than 130 miles south of the 49th Parallel.)

The negotiators agreed to use as the border the winding path of rivers and lakes from Lake Superior to Lake of the Woods, which was the main route of the *voyageurs*, the French-Canadian and increasingly part-Indian canoeists who muscled the fur trade. From Montreal to Lake Huron the principal route was in present-day Canada, shortcutting today's International Boundary, through a series of rivers into Georgian Bay of Lake Huron. From Lake Huron the Great Lakes route was due west, often with a stopover at Mackinac Island for refurbishing and food supplies, then through the Sault St. Marie into Lake Superior. (This route avoided the much longer way through Lakes Ontario and Erie, and most of Lake Huron itself.) Goods were backpacked nine miles uphill, bypassing the rapids and waterfalls of the Pigeon River. Then 25-foot canoes transported them through the wild country to trading posts set up when French explorers were searching for riches and a northwest passage in the 1600s. The posts reached into the interior to the Rockies, Athabasca, and Hudson Bay. Prairie buffalo hunters prepared and sold pemmican to them in bulk, and furs were brought in by the local Indians. The voyageur route was 3,000 miles from Montreal to the Athabasca area, and eventually it stretched farther in the search for furs.

The treaty negotiators established one of the world's most unusual borders between nations. From the mouth of the Pigeon River to the Lake of the Woods the border was the "customary" route of the fur trade, which in 1842 was still brisk. The negotiating teams indulged in a last round of disagreement. The British claimed that the "customary" route began near Duluth, Minnesota, at Fond du Lac and wound north to Rainy Lake. Not so, the Americans countered; the "customary" route began at Thunder Bay, Ontario (then Ft. William) and followed the rivers and lakes west to Rainy Lake. The difference was thousands of square miles including portions of the then unknown Mesabi Iron Range. It was finally set at about midpoint, which was not compromise but yielding to fact. The main route *was* the one from Grand Portage and had been the most heavily traveled course of the fur trade for about 150 years. Although it was not known until recently, this had also been a main route for Copper Culture and Woodland Indians for perhaps 8,000 years before the days of the fur trade.

The Webster-Ashburton Treaty—so called for the principal negotiators, Daniel Webster for the Americans and Lord Ashburton for the British—named the major lakes and rivers between Grand Portage and "the most north western point of the Lake of the Woods" and went on to specify that it would be "understood that all water communications and all the usual portages . . . as now actually used, shall be free and open to the use of the citizens . . . of both countries." And they still are, though the final survey was not finished and published until 1931. There is an International Joint Commission with jurisdiction over the boundary waters, which played a vital role in preserving the ecological integrity and future of the area when twentieth-century entrepreneurs wanted to flood major portions to build power dams. The Mississippi's source is well within the United States, and the natural avenues and riverways leading to the northwest are as safely in Canada.

Today's voyageur and tourist approaches the park through country that is breathtakingly evocative of the way it was in Indian and fur-trade days, through mile after mile of forest, peat bog, and tundra-like marsh; along countless lakes, rivers, ancient rock formations, and hills. Two highways fed by the interstate system lead to International Falls, 11 miles from the park: one from Duluth, 175 miles southeast, the other from Minneapolis-St. Paul, 350 miles south by way of Brainerd and Bemidji. A smaller all-weather state road leading west from International Falls closely follows the Rainy River to Lake of the Woods 100 miles away. At International Falls an archaic, privately owned bridge spans the

Rainy River and connects with the Canadian sister city of Ft. Frances, the transcanada highway system, and railroad.

Air travelers arrive in International Falls from Duluth or Minneapolis-St. Paul, or fly from Winnipeg to Ft. Frances on daily commercial flights. One popular airline's emblem is a flying goose; the carrier has one of the best safety records in America. This is reassuring to visitors who experience occasional air turbulence, look at the two engines, and then down at the seemingly endless expanse of forest, lakes, and rivers, broken only rarely by small villages and scattered farms. In the 30-mile periphery of the park there are fewer than 200 small farms, which are congregated around the little towns of Orr and Littlefork. There are more resorts than farms, and it is customary for resort operators to meet incoming planes to pick up fishermen and vacationers. The rail lines to International Falls have become freight carriers, but if ecology-conscious Americans ever resume rail travel as a national mode, it would provide an ironic touch, for the railroad to International Falls was built by those who wanted to exploit timber and water resources in the early 1900s, in order to establish an industrial empire in the northwoods.

Voyageurs Park is 344 square miles, about 219,000 acres, of which nearly half is water. It exists in a wilderness context of thousands of square miles. Most of the land around it is still left to wildlife and pulpwood operations because so far it has proved unsuited or unprofitable for anything else—or investors have thought of it as too remote to develop. Some park visitors still come by canoe, in the same fashion and through the same waterways and landscapes as did the voyageurs, the fur traders, and the Indians before them. Canoeists are using the park in increasing numbers for several reasons. In summer the remoter parts of the park are otherwise inaccessible, and it is adjacent to the Superior National Forest, which contains the famous Boundary Waters Canoe Area (BWCA), a protected wilderness 150 miles from Grand Portage to Voyageurs, with only a few controlled access roads into the area. The number of persons issued entry permits to BWCA has had to be limited. Canoeing, camping, and hiking have become so popular that it is necessary to cushion the unintentional impact of these visitors on the wilderness they love.

Unlike the BWCA's network of rivers, lakes, gorges, rapids, and waterfalls in a rock-and-forest setting where the panorama is busy and sometimes cramped, Voyageurs is vast and has much open space. It is dominated by four large lakes and their myriad rocky islands. Three of the lakes—Rainy, Namakan, and Kabetogama—shelter a roadless peninsula, Kabetogama, of over 100,000 acres. The fourth, Sand Point Lake, feeds into the Namakan. This is picturesque and occasionally dangerous country. The huge lakes respond quickly to winds so that within minutes after a storm comes up even motorboats have to seek shelter in one of the many cliff-sided bays and inlets.

Attempting to cross Rainy Lake in a storm is foolhardy. The lake is over 35 miles from Kettle Falls at the east where Namakan spills into it, to Koochiching Falls on the west where International Falls and Ft. Frances stand today. The Rainy Lake islands are so situated that no wind-safe channel can be found during some storms. Fur traders complained in their journals of being windbound. They used the time to patch canoes with extra gum and birchbark, to cook and eat in a leisurely fashion, a departure from hurried meals during the customary 18-hour-day while en route. They tried to make up the lost time by night travel.

The Kabetogama peninsula is over 30 miles from tip to end and in places 6 miles across. It contains several lakes, one a major muskellunge spawning site, and active beaver ponds. It is a haven for flora and fauna, shielded from humans who can reach it only by crossing water or winter ice undercut by currents where Kabetogama and the mainland reach toward each other.

The peninsula is an irregularly shaped land mass. Rocky rolling hills stretch to the horizon in all directions when viewed from a hilltop at the center. It is irregularly reforested by natural regrowth after turn-of-the-century logging and fires. Some of the hills dip down to sloughs and beaver ponds, rise again to bare outcroppings covered with lichens, a favorite food of the woodland caribou who used to graze here. Some of the lakes can be reached by portage and canoe, others only on foot. Winter snowshoe and ski trails skirt dense brush, wind through a few stands of large, older trees, and are crossed by countless game trails. Those who relish tracking and identifying animal spoors find ideal conditions on Kabetogama.

The peninsula rock of biotite, quartz, and feldspar schist contains intrusions of many-hued granites. These rock formations, like others throughout the park, contain sedimentary remains of the four- to five-billion-year-old original earth mantle, or crust. Elsewhere in the United States this ancient rock is covered by hundreds and thousands of feet of accumulated debris, the result of weathering erosion, upheavals, and ancient lake deposits. Here this accumulation was scraped away by the glaciers. It is the largest display of remains of the original earth crust in the United States, the southern tip of the Precambrian Shield, revealed by the retreating Ice Age. The shield spreads northward in Canada to the arctic. Since the glaciers that scooped out the lakes and bared the landscape were the last ones on the continent, and disappeared about 13,000 years ago, Voyageurs Park displays some of the world's oldest geologic formations and some of its newest—the Precambrian and the postglacial.

The northwest tip of Kabetogama dips to Rainy Lake at the Black Bay Narrows, the bay spreading southward. Offshore in Rainy Lake are the islands where ancient greenstone emerges at the earth's surface—here gold was discovered in 1893. The find led to a frontier-type rush and the overnight eruption of Rainy Lake City on the peninsula as adventurers, goldseekers, and their ancillaries swooped down. By 1894 there were mining rigs, steamboats, and a town of 500. Rainy Lake lasted six years, which was longer than the life-span of the gold mines. There are few signs of the town now. At the turn of the century, departing residents hauled away everything that could be used, including some of the houses and most building materials, and helped to establish the new town of Koochiching 11 miles west. Koochiching was eventually renamed International Falls. Some years later even the gold-mine tailings were hauled away by barge and used as underlayment for the streets of International Falls. Legends of Rainy Lake City live on even though the forest has reasserted itself on the site of the old town.

Today the citizens of International Falls joke that their streets are paved with gold, but the real sources of employment and wealth are wood products, paper production, and logging. The town of 10,000 is sited where a fur-trading post once stood; at different times there were posts across the river at Ft. Frances and down-stream. French, English, and American traders had situated at or near the Koochiching Falls from the 1600s to the middle 1800s. For a time Rainy Lake posts were major depots where goods were delivered in bulk and then fanned out to the brigades from the far interior. The Athabasca brigades, for instance, had difficulty making the round trip to Grand Portage between breakup and freezeup. Inevitably the Rainy Lake area was the scene of conflict and violence between rival fur-trade companies.

Ft. Frances, where the Hudson's Bay Company post stood in the early 1800s, was named for the bride of George Simpson, a governor of the company, who brought Frances along on his annual voyage from Montreal to Winnipeg in 1830, the first official to bring a wife. This enchanted the voyageurs who paddled Simpson and the post's company clerks and they made a ceremony of the visit. Simpson traveled the route with a hand-picked crew of voyageurs and made it a point to set speed records on his trips, knowing that the regular brigades would try to match or beat his time; voyageurs were a competitive lot. Simpson traveled light, but the voyageurs had to haul cargo and no one is known to have bettered him. Tall beaver hat perched squarely on his head, Simpson would sit erect in the canoe seeming undaunted by rapids and waterfalls, and merely in a hurry to do his business. His wife was along when, one year, he bade his crew take a hazardous shortcut, shooting most of the rapids of the Namakan River. Nothing to it, he reassured the contract canoeists, much shorter and easier; but in this instance they did not follow his lead.

Along the picturesque north shore of Kabetogama Peninsula is the 35-mile east-west stretch of Rainy Lake. The International Boundary courses through the center of the lake, winding betwixt islands, through the Brule Narrows, then straight down the great open stretch to the east tip and Kettle Falls.

At the southwest the peninsula is connected to the mainland by a narrow but hilly neck of land between Black Bay and Lake Kabetogama. To map readers it might seem that this land bridge of a mile or so would have been a shortcut for the voyageurs. However, they preferred paddling to portaging. The same was true at Kettle Falls, where a shorter channel from Namakan Lake into Rainy Lake involved two or three portages, depending on water level, and some of the brigades took the longer way that had but one portage. The land bridge from Black Bay to Kabetogama was used only rarely in the fur trade, but it had prolonged use by Indians for whom the Kabetogama area provided campsites, berries, game, and fish for several thousand years. Lake Kabetogama forms the southern coast of the peninsula. Like Namakan Lake, into which it empties, and Rainy Lake, it runs generally east-west. The current, however, flows east into Namakan and through it, then west in Rainy Lake.

Lakes have unique personalities and character, manifesting a range of moods which mirror seasons and conditions. All bodies of water reflect the peach, mauve, and scarlet of sunset, the autumn colors and shades of winter whites, but each imbues them with its own imprint. The canoeist traveling the border lakes and passing through many in rapid succession is very aware of this and treasures the gems of a voyage. Laconic as some of the fur traders' journals were, a loving tone creeps in when they refer to Saganaga, for instance, in the BWCA, and to some of the others. Kabetogama is such a lake.

The aesthetic pleasure stems from several sources. Foremost is probably the vista of odd-shaped granite islands. Most have trees and berry patches, and a few lend themselves to camping, though small islands have a low tolerance for even careful users. A rule of thumb for mainland campsites is that two years of reasonable use require five years of recuperation; an island ecosystem is less resilient. Backdropping the islands are the irregularly shaped coves, inlets, and bays of the peninsula, behind which rise the rolling massif and silhouette of the hills. Although the forest is no longer predominantly big pine, it is a lovely mixed forest including aspen, birch, pine, spruce, and other species. Along the south shore of Lake Kabetogama looms the excrudescence of the Vermilion Batholith. A batholith is a large igneous mass that intruded, cooled, and crystallized at great depth long ago. It usually has steep walls and a domed roof. The Vermilion Batholith underlies an area 35 miles wide and 80 miles long in northern Minnesota and is the largest body of granite rocks exposed in the state. This ridge is crossed by the two access roads in the park, one of them at Kabetogama.

It was at the west end of the lake that the Ojibway Chief Wooden Frog maintained his village and band into the 1930s, even though the Bois Forte Ojibway (Deep Woods Ojibway) had lost the vast bulk of their territory in the treaties of 1854 and 1866. The latter provided for a reservation at Nett Lake, 35 miles south of Kabetogama and, in 1866, called Netor Assabacona; it also promised one township on the "Grand Fork River" to be "at the mouth of Deer Creek, if such location shall be found practicable." The township was later "taken" by a logging company. The other benefits were temporary and minor, coming to less than $20,000. In return the Bois Fort Indians were to give up all territory in the border country from Lake Vermilion west and move to the reservation. Most did, for at least some portion of each year. Nett Lake today is a tough, proud community on one of the best wild-rice lakes in the north. Wooden Frog lived where he liked it best, usually outside the manmade reservation boundary on Kabetogama, sometimes visiting Nett Lake.

On the southwest shore of Kabetogama Lake the park boundaries follow the lakeshore for several miles, then exclude land on which several resorts are located, to provide the park visitors with accommodations and to illustrate how the park would economically benefit the surrounding, sometimes depressed and always marginal, community. When national park legislation for Voyageurs was being considered, local sentiment was divided. Some saw the park as an economic and environmental boon, others opposed it as interfering with hunting, fishing, timbering, and snowmobiling. The decision to retain the few Kabetogama resorts in the southwest, and some others at the west end of the park at Ash River and to exclude Crane Lake itself with its resorts and commercial facilities was a compromise ensuring wider local support of the park proposal and easing the pains of ultimate passage. The resorts, none of them large, are nestled among the trees and granite of the shore and its bays.

Kabetogama, island-studded, narrows at the east to flow into

Namakan Lake. Just before entering the narrow channel into Namakan there is another channel to the south, Ash River, leading to Sullivan Bay. This narrow bay, amid granite cliffs, is nearly three miles east to west and is the terminus of the second road into the park. Some would have it that the Ash River and Namakan match or exceed the beauty of Kabetogama. *Chacun à son goût.*

To voyageurs bringing in trade goods, the arrival at Kettle Falls meant an end to numerous, rough portages, sometimes several in short succession. Whatever their destination, from here on there would still be portages, some of them quite hard, but nothing to compare with what they had passed on their way from Grand Portage to Sand Point Lake, the east boundary of the park. Ordinarily this segment took 10 days, first ascending the height of land that divides the Lake Superior basin from the Rainy Lake / Hudson Bay basin. A 1737 account listed 47 portages between Grand Portage and Rainy Lake, others cited figures of 30 to 40. Between Rainy Lake and Winnipeg there were 20 to 30. The exact number varied according to the prevailing water level. High water sometimes enabled canoeists to shoot a rapids that in low water had to be roped, poled, or portaged. When roping a canoe, men along shore used guide and tow ropes and a long stick to keep the craft in the current; when poling a canoe, two or more with long poles stood in the canoe, usually one in the bow and one in the stern, to propel the craft up or down stream. Each portage required carrying the several thousand pounds of goods, or furs on the return trip, packed into 90-pound bales. The bales were supported by tump lines around the voyageur's forehead, his hands holding the bottom of the bale. Often two or more bales were carried at a time, and the men competed to see who could carry the heaviest loads fastest and farthest. Carrying less and making more trips back and forth over the portage trail meant paddling later into the night. The customary work hours for voyageurs en route do not compare to those of today's typical vacationing canoeist. The brigade, in three or more canoes, would often rouse at 4 or 5 A.M., taking advantage of the long northern day. After a hurried breakfast they would paddle and portage until late evening, have another hasty meal at about 9 or 10, and then sleep. Hourly *pipes*, or rest stops, were called during the day for smoking a clay pipe of tobacco. On a long portage the rests were *poses*, regular intervals for resting the load on a rack. During *poses* on very long portages, loads were taken off and the men returned to the starting point for other loads, leapfrogging the first pile of bales to the second *pose*, returning empty for the first and taking it to the third, and so on. Carrying the canoe was an easier portion of this grueling work.

The principal occupational disease of voyageurs was strangulated hernia, not drowning, freezing, starving, or violence. The occupational disease of the European hatters who manufactured the furs into fashionable felt hats was madness, for the microscopic fibers released in the conversion process were breathed in, absorbed, and ultimately could lead to the insanity that gave birth to the expression "mad as a hatter." For the Indians who supplied most of the furs, the trade meant not only conversion to commercialism and Christianity, but also surrender of a seasonally oriented life cycle in balance with the natural environment, resulting in the loss of their form of civilization and a workable culture, loss of their spiritual system and internal civil order, and ultimately removal from the land.

The voyageurs were willing to take calculated risks and shot some rapids to save portaging time. Portaging then, as now, is brutally hard, and sometimes packs split, goods were lost or damaged or left behind. Shooting rapids is quick, a matter of skill and strength. Mishaps did occur, as skindiving archaeologists have discovered, recovering nested brass kettles and other trade goods. Since the voyageurs' mode of travel through the beautiful terrain was so demanding, they tried every possible shortcut, although common sense should have indicated that if workable shortcuts existed, the Indians would have found them over a period of several thousand years. The Namakan route would have eliminated the long loop of today's international border from Lac La Croix around Loon and Little Vermilion Lakes to Sand Point Lake. But, as indicated earlier, there were more portages and infinitely more risks on the Namakan River. Today this route is considered one of the more challenging and difficult routes and is recommended only for expert canoeists. Another shortcut was created much later, when the fur trade was waning, immigrants were paying voyageurs to transport them to the interior, and the first small steamboats were appearing on the larger lakes (some lakes were dammed to aid navigation). This shortcut was the 4-mile-long Dawson Trail portage from Lac La Croix into Sand Point Lake, which is still extant.

Around the corner to the left of the traditional voyageur entry into Sand Point Lake there is a narrow channel leading south to Crane Lake. This is where the southern route from Fond du Lac, which in 1842 the British and Canadians had claimed was the "customary" one, emerged. This route led up the St. Louis River, over the watershed and into Lake Vermilion, down the Vermilion River to Crane Lake, and then joined the trunk highway where Crane Lake empties into Sand Point. It sounds short but it wasn't, either in miles or in portages. Among its obstacles is a series of waterfalls, rapids, and a gorge about two miles up the Vermilion River from Crane Lake, as dramatic today as ever, and referred to as a *detroit*, or narrow sluice, in the old journals. Below the detroit of the Vermilion River and just before coming out on Crane Lake there is a quiet cove sheltered by cliffs where one of the first trading posts in the area was erected by Rene Bourassa in 1736 when he was "wintered in." The little post was stockaded because it traded with the Ojibway who at the time were involved in a long territorial war with the Sioux. The post was used only briefly and later trading posts were erected nearby. The northern route, which in 1842 the Americans had claimed to be the customary one, went from Ft. William and joined the trunk highway farther to the east, at Lac La Croix.

From Sand Point Lake on, all routes combined and led through the lake, north past the islands clustering around the exit, and through the Namakan Narrows. Most of the way through these narrows on the east cliff are Indian pictographs of moose, people in canoes, suns, and footprints. Two of the pictographs are white, the only such on the highway, where the standard pigment is red or reddish-brown. Indians apparently regarded the snakelike fold of pink feldspar in the mica slate cliff as a water manitou, or spirit, manifestation and added their artistic manitous to the one provided by nature. The white pigment was made of sturgeon oil and a chalky rock found below the narrows. One slab containing pictographs was removed a few years ago when in danger of separating from the cliff and falling into the water; it is now in Toronto's Royal Museum.

Beyond the narrows and a group of guardian islands, Namakan Lake opens in a stretch of nearly four miles. About midway is Gull Island, which at a distance looks iridescent, chalky white; it is denuded by nesting herring gulls. Now as then canoeists stick to the longer east shore when the wind is blowing or find shelter if the wind is very strong, for the wind funnels through the rock formations of the shore and quickly whips the lake into whitecaps. On the east shore of Namakan the Namakan River quietly empties, belying the hazardous course from Lac La Croix. In the Namakan River (called Namah, or sturgeon, by the Indians) the Indians built fish-spearing platforms out 20 feet or more. They stood motionless, spear in hand. Sturgeon, an ancient boneless fish, grew to 12 feet, and catches in excess of 100 pounds were not uncommon. Voyageurs would stop to trade for fish, berries, and meat, since their travel tempo did not allow time for fishing and hunting.

Voyageurs could choose one of several routes from Namakan to Rainy Lake. Today it is thought that most brigades left Namakan by way of Bear River, about three miles southeast of Kettle Falls. Some fur-trade diaries refer to the next channel up the line, nearly as short but requiring two portages; others went the longer Kettle Falls way, with one portage. Perhaps if the 1842 treaty negotiators had made the trip themselves, they would have set the international boundary at Bear River. This is one of several anomalies or vagaries in the "customary route." The boundary was put at Kettle Falls, for better or worse, which is named for rock on the sides of the falls hollowed out in the shape of kettles by water-twirled boulders.

Today there is a turn-of-the-century hostel at Kettle Falls—with an old nickelodeon in working condition and the original decor— which has been listed on the National Register of Historic Places. The hostel came into being after the fur trade had died away and when loggers, commercial fishermen, and dam construction workers congregated in the early 1900s. About 200 people made up a temporary community at Kettle Falls, and it was rumored that the money to build the hostel came from members of the oldest profession who had come to the northwoods to ply their trade. Only the hostel is left now, and nature has reclaimed the land as it has the former site of Rainy Lake City. The Park Service maintains the Kettle Falls Hotel.

It may seem incongruous that the peaceful, often arcadian setting of Voyageurs was the scene of such varied, sometimes violent, activity by nature and by man. The rugged character of the parkland exhibits the most ancient shell of the earth and its newest geological creations. The animal occupants have included the extinct mammoth, mastodon, and giant bison; elk and caribou predominated and were driven out, but may be reintroduced. A wide spectrum of flora and fauna still thrives in the land. It has been host to the earliest Americans and their descendants, perhaps in preglacial times and certainly from the time the last glaciers disappeared to the present. It has survived as a viable, if fragile, ecosystem despite the excesses of mankind and because of the caring of mankind. *Vita brevis, munda longa.*

2

Geological Time

About 10,000 years ago there was a huge lake where the park is today. People then looked much as they do today, and animals were much as they are today, although some are now extinct and have to be recreated out of plaster in museums. If we go back about 18,000 years, we encounter a time when mile-high glaciers reached down Canada from the Arctic, spreading tongues and fingers into America's midland. With effort we can imagine those glaciers shrinking, enlarging, and shrinking again as weather cycles of thousands of years heated and chilled the world. But sooner or later going back in time begins to boggle the mind. There is nothing we can identify with when we think of the first single-celled creatures in the sea about 600 million years ago. From this time back to the first cooling and solidification of the earth's molten surface nearly 5 billion years ago is called the Precambrian. It is difficult to conceive of times so far removed, although space-age experiences enable us, in our mind's eye, to view the world from outer space and imagine it a fiery ball; and we can take our cocooned psyches to a park and look not only at the beauties there, but also at the evidence and remnants of the beginnings of the earth's natural history.

From the time that it cooled and hardened, the earth crust began to be covered over. Volcanoes erupted and spewed lava, volcanic flows penetrated weak spots and fissures, and spread over parts of the earth's surface. Oceans covered it all, and sediments sifted down, were buried by other sediments, and eventually hardened. Mountains were pushed up and then peneplaned, mostly by running water, by freezing and thawing. Runoff waters carved valleys and carried debris. This weathering process broke up rock formations, producing even smaller debris some of which became components of sand and soil. Time and again these processes occurred, covering much of the original crust with hundreds and thousands of feet of accumulation.

It seems inconceivable that mountains should rise, then be planed to undulating landscape by streams. That oceans should come into being so that huge landmasses are awash. That molten rock should spew from the interior of the earth, or flow out in large quantities through fractures and fissures, and that this rock should in turn cool, harden, and be eroded by water and weathering. Little is known about the very first earth mantle and about all the sequences and cataclysms that occurred during Precambrian times, a span of about 4 billion years. Very little fossil evidence exists in Precambrian rocks to help establish the dates of events, and only in recent years has the advent of radiometric dating begun to open the door to a better understanding of this seven-eighths of the earth's history.

At one point in Precambrian times, between 1 and 2 billion years ago, Minnesota was a center of episodes of violent volcanic activity, perhaps among the greatest the earth experienced. Northern Minnesota was covered by inland seas, and lava flowed beneath the water and on the exposed land. One residue of this is the pillowing of lava; there is a very small sample in the park and other samples between the park and International Falls. Much later the

Lake Superior basin was essentially created by subsiding of the earth crust and tilt of the basin to the southeast.

Fracture lines in the rock formations indicate repeated shifts and settlings of the crust after the volcanism. This can be seen in the cliffs and shoreline of Lake Superior and farther inland. Near the south edge of the park the east-west ridge of the Vermilion Batholith provides a panoramic view of the lakes. The granite mass is crossed by overland visitors since both roads into the park, at Kabetogama and Ash River, have to traverse it before descending to the lakes. The Vermilion Batholith is about 80 miles long, formed by igneous material deep underground.

At the north edge of the park a belt of greenstone is exposed. It emerges from the water on the north of Kabetogama Peninsula, on Dryweed and Big American Islands and the small islands between the two and the mainland at Neil Point. The greenstone pops up along the north edge of the park and dips under Rainy Lake, then trails west and north in Canada shortly after leaving the park. On the U.S. mainland it meanders west-north-west along the border lakes and rivers, occasionally visible, at other times underground or underwater. It is in the greenstone that turn-of-the-century prospectors found small amounts of gold and traces of silver, copper, and platinum-group metals. As one of the oldest rock formations, and the most likely one for mineral deposits, the greenstone belt has long been probed by gold seekers and mining companies. In recent years, prospecting and drilling teams have been traveling the Boundary Waters and Superior Forest areas to test for deposits of nickel, copper, and other valuable ores. Some of the outfitters and environmentalists have speculated that the real motive for improving the Gunflint Trail, one of the few roads into the Boundary Waters, was to facilitate prospecting and potential mining. The Gunflint Trail was proverbial as one of the roughest roads in America, dipping and curving over rock ridges and down through potholes and swamps; one really had to have a very strong desire to go canoeing or get into the back country to use it. Since the 1960s it has been graded, widened, and paved, and nature lovers nervously watch the car culture and commercial use of what used to be a backwoodsman's test of mettle.

The Ice Age, or Pleistocene Era, began about 2 million years ago and lasted until recent times, about 10 or 15 thousand years ago. During the interval between the Precambrian and Pleistocene eras most life forms we know, and which produced us, came into being.

During Pleistocene times (and perhaps even before) large glacial masses formed and covered much of North America. (Three older glaciations have been dated at 700, 400, and 270 million years ago; all lasted a long time and were widely separated in time. For reasons not entirely clear now, some major glaciations were marked by repeated growth and shrinking. It appears that each time the more recent Pleistocene glaciers retreated, vegetation and animals occupied the terrain, moving in quickly in the same warm-weather rush that contributed to the disappearance of the glacier. Presumably over the long stretch of the Pleistocene, each succeeding inrush of flora and fauna was more complex and varied, better able to adapt and survive. During the last glaciation, which finally disappeared about 13,000 years ago, there were at least four major glacial advances that tongued down from the north and over the park area.

Glaciers form over a long period when more snow falls than melts. The surface melts and refreezes, and weight accumulates and compacts the mass. Snowflakes turn into corn snow and become denser below the surface. Under very great pressure, ice acts like a viscous liquid below surface depths, contributing to the flow of ice sheets over virtually any terrain, depending on the thickness of the ice. The great weight of glaciers sometimes pressed down the earth crust, which would spring back after the glaciers had gone. Some of the Lake Superior basin, for example, was depressed in this fashion and is still "springing back" at the rate of a few millimeters a year.

Glaciers moving over bedrock can pick up large rocks and embed them in the ice. The rocks abrade and mark the bedrock. Loosened rocks above the glacier roll or tumble on it and become a part of it, contributing to the debris that is left behind when the glacier ultimately melts entirely.

The complex workings of the glaciers produced a generally undulating and rounded topography, the remaining bedrock marked by striations and gouges, the farther edges cluttered with debris, dumped as the ice finally melted. The glacial dumps were subjected to the workings of running water as tremendous amounts of freshwater were released by the melt. It is estimated that when glaciation was at a peak, ocean levels went down about 300 to 500 feet. One of the byproducts of this drop in sea level, in all likelihood, was the exposure of the land bridge from Asia to America at the Bering Straits, over which early Americans entered the continent. The arrival of the first humans in America is continually being pushed back as archaeological discoveries are made. The current estimate is between 40,000 and 70,000 years ago, shifting to the later date. It is probable that the first humans arrived in Minnesota before the last glaciers disappeared, judging from the find of Clovis-type points associated with the period at Browns Valley, which was near the southern edge of the last glacial tongue to reach down into Minnesota. Humans followed the migrating mammoth and other large game, which found their way to the interior of the continent, including the park area.

The final retreat of the glacial finger that covered the park is estimated at 13,000 years ago, some scientists fixing the time closer to 10,000. As the glacier melted, water built up into a huge lake blocked at the north by the receding ice. This was the second glacial Lake Agassiz—much evidence of the prior glaciation and Agassiz I has been overridden by Agassiz II. This temporary lake is thought to have been the largest freshwater lake that ever existed on the North American continent, covering much of northern Minnesota and North Dakota, and stretching far into Canada. The lake beaches can be seen in the park and as far away as the Dakotas and central Canada. The beach gravel and pebbles are not worn round as they would be if Lake Agassiz had existed longer.

The lake was named for Swiss naturalist Louis Agassiz. Agassiz, among his other contributions to human knowledge, formulated and defined the concept of continental glaciation, glacial movement, and dumping. He had observed nonstratified gravel and deduced its origin as glacial moraine. Agassiz came to the United States to lecture in 1846, subsequently taught at Harvard and spent the second half of his life here. He is still considered one of the ablest science teachers the country has known, teaching as he practiced that "if you study nature in books, when you go out of doors you cannot find her. . . . The book of nature is always open." He preferred to give his students field experience and through such experience to have them gather and interpret facts. Most notable natural-history teachers in the latter half of the nineteenth century were Agassiz pupils and co-workers.

Lake Agassiz must have been a stunning sight for prehistoric people hunting big game to its edges. At its peak it was several hundred miles across in any direction. Here and there rocky islands protruded as the lake level receded by stages, flora establishing itself on the little outcroppings. There has been speculation that when neolithic hunters saw this body of water, it was a vast milky white expanse, comparable to glacial runoff or *gletscher milch*. This probably was not so. Small glacial lakes become turquoise or milky white as melting progresses and ground-up rock flour is fed in by glacial streams. This sediment sinks to the bottom and can be stirred up by wind and waves. Dr. John A. Elson of McGill University, an authority on Lake Agassiz, doubts that it was milky white except within a few miles of the margin, if there, since the milk entered at the bottom and the lake at its peak was several hundred feet deep.

The area of Lake Agassiz exceeded that of the combined Great Lakes. The dammed up glacial melt, increasing in volume and blocked on the north by the slowly disappearing wall of ice, carved a temporary outlet, and a torrent of water rushed down the Minnesota River and the Mississippi, widening valleys, steepening bluffs, and shearing off headlands. Eventually Agassiz carved other outlets as well, into Lake Superior near Nipigon, and later to the far northwest and the Mackenzie River basin. When enough ice had melted to the north, drainage into Hudson Bay resumed and the torrential source of the Minnesota River was beheaded and assumed its present form, a marsh dividing its trickling headwaters from those of the Red River of the North that flows to Winnipeg and thence to Hudson Bay. The bequests of Lake Agassiz include the rich soil of the Red River Valley, Lake Winnipeg and the border lakes. In addition, the lake caused the dispersal of a wide variety of molluscan fauna and fish. Where the environment is hospitable, fish extend their territory at the rate of 20 to 40 miles a year. Lake Agassiz accelerated this process, and when the lake receded, leaving separate watersheds, the fish varieties had been scattered.

When Lake Agassiz disappeared, the warm climate literally exploded the forest into the newly vacated land. Aspen and pine, crowding the edge of the receding glacier and lakeshores, rooted where upland emerged; spruce and a wide range of marsh vegetation moved into the lowlands, for Agassiz had bestowed sediment there. Among the higher rocks, trees took hold in cracks and fissures, in dumps of glacial moraine, the mounds and piles of gravel, sand, and soil left behind.

Glaciers dumped the geologic accumulation of millions of years on midland America and left exposed a huge expanse of the earth's crust from Canada's north into Minnesota and the entire Lake Superior region. Geologists consider it the largest outcropping of Precambrian rock in the United States. The geologic history of the Middle and Late Precambrian era cannot be found in the park, for that accumulation was bestowed on the lands to the south. What we do see in the park is a rare display of the nucleus of the North American continent, the Precambrian Shield, present in the vivid colors of the rocks: browns, greens, blacks, contrasting with grays, and reds, marked by bright veins of white and pink quartz. There are dramatic rock formations and lakes, bounded in the park by the greenstone belt at the north and the Vermilion Batholith on the south. Farther south are the first glacial moraines. And although the elevations are not very great, from lake bottoms to hilltops they rarely exceed 300 feet, the matrix of granite cliffs, boreal forest and marsh, and the webwork of interconnecting lakes and rivers provide a mix of the most recent geologically, the postglacial, and the most ancient, the Precambrian.

This is a unique land and waterscape of islands and sheer cliffs, of sheltered bays and windswept lakes. The combination of open space and sheltering islands is comparable to some parts of the Aegean Sea. Like the Aegean, this land was not very fertile and not always hospitable, but it attracted humans by its beauty. Actually the attraction was practical as well as aesthetic, the islands providing safety and the current and wind providing passage between watersheds. It is still a matter of speculation whether neolithic Americans were in the area before the last glacier intruded, but clearly humans have traveled, lived, and found spiritual as well as physical contentment there since.

3

People of Canoe, Copper, and Wild Rice

The reconstructed Grand Portage stockade and voyageurs hall, where in the days of the fur trade the annual rendezvous brought together brigades and trade officials from the interior and from Montreal, now houses a museum. One of the exhibits is a slab of rock weighing several hundred pounds that was removed from the nine-mile trail of the Grand Portage, the great or long carry. The granite is deeply worn in the middle, stepped down by the feet of human travelers. The fur traders attempted using oxen, carts, and horses to save the men the lugging of 180 pounds or more at a carry. But the terrain was too rough and all trade goods had to be backpacked over hill and through marsh to Ft. Charlotte on the Pigeon River, and the fur bales from the interior had to be backpacked on the return to Grand Portage. During the 150 years of the heavy fur-trade traffic, many thousands of people used this trail, which is now a National Monument administered by the Park

Service. The traffic included author Washington Irving, who came to see the famous place and write about it and about the explorers, Hudson's Bay governors, and adventurers, as well as the sturdy little French Canadians who made up the bulk of the voyageurs' ranks. The slab had been worn down before they all arrived. The Grand Portage, and the other portages of the north country and of the continent, had been used for several thousand years.

The ancient trails crossed the heights of land between watersheds, facilitating travel between the Great Lakes, the Mississippi, Hudson's Bay, and the far west and northwest to the Rockies, Athabasca, and the Mackenzie River. They led around the waterway obstacles of rapids, falls, and gorges by the best available route.

We are becoming increasingly informed about the incredible distances traveled by early Americans. Yet virtually no trace has been found of the old-world language stock among the 500 or so Indian languages and dialects. There is only speculation that from about 35,000 until 10,000 years ago, the sparse population was fairly homogeneous, scattering in its hunt of camel, ground sloth, tapir, mammoth, horse, mastodon, elk, caribou, giant beaver, and bison. Diversification was probably heightened between 8,000 and 1,500 years ago, when diminishing herds made the Indians less reliant on hunting, and more reliant on gathering wild fruits, vegetables, and rice, and eventually on agriculture.

It is also uncertain just when Indians invented the canoe, or whether dugouts were used before the light-weight, maneuverable birchbark canoes were devised. The canoe made long distance travel and commerce possible for the Indians, and was almost certainly in use by the time of the Copper Culture 5,000 years ago, and perhaps before. The birchbark canoe is regarded as one of humankind's more ingenious and beneficial inventions, a use of native materials that produced a unique craft. Without the canoe, travel in this terrain would have been virtually impossible in the summer, and it is questionable whether humans would have had much success earning a livelihood and would have been able to scatter and settle over such wide areas in a relatively short time and then establish a commercial life.

A skeleton found about 10 feet below the surface during a 1931 road excavation in west-central Minnesota's Otter Trail County is probably 12,000 years old. Although the site was disturbed, it appears to have come from the lake bottom of a glacial lake older than Agassiz. The skeleton has raised many questions. Nicknamed 'Minnesota Man', it was determined to be that of a young woman. With the skeleton were found a knife made of elk antler and a conch shell, which presumably could have come from no nearer than the Gulf of Mexico. It appears the young woman drowned, perhaps while crossing the winter ice of the glacial lake.

Even older than the skeleton were the fluted Clovis and Folsom points, trademarks of prehistoric mammoth and bison hunters of the great plains. (A Clovis point embedded in a giant bison skull provided one of the first leads to the length of time early Americans had lived in North America.) These stone spearpoints are grooved on both sides; the names derive from the New Mexico sites where they were first found, although these weapons have since been discovered through much of the midcontinent. The time of the nomadic big-game hunters is now being put in the range of 70,000 B.C. to the postglacial period. But the trend in archaeology, as discoveries accumulate, has been to push the time of the first Americans back into the Pleistocene. Since the glaciers destroyed much of the prehistoric evidence, researchers dream of finding a cave in the north country that survived the glaciers and has embedded in the layers of its floor the clear traces of humans. It is not likely that this dream will come true, because the rock formations do not lend themselves to the existence of caves. But more information becomes available each year, and recently low water in the park unexpectedly revealed prehistoric artifacts.

A significant paleo-Indian site has been uncovered at Browns Valley in western Minnesota, helping to illuminate the life of these early big-game hunters. We have learned that they made finely crafted tools from flint, chalcedony, and chert; they used fire, lived in small groups, and were widely distributed over the habitable areas. Were they alive today, they would be recognizable as American Indians.

Archaeologists have been able to establish more about the people since 8,000 B.C. and how they lived. At the beginning of this period—which for several thousand years hence was called the Eastern Archaic Tradition—the parkland started to look much as it does today. New tools came into use as humans learned to grind and peck stone implements, in addition to chipping them. Woodworking tools became finer, and copper tools, weapons, and ornaments came into use. With a few exceptions, the copper was mined at Isle Royale and then transported in chunks for manufacture back home, although sometimes the miners did their manufacturing while camped on the island or immediately on their return to the mainland. Isle Royale copper has been traced considerable distances, and was traded or transported in a radius of many hundreds of miles into Canada and mid-America. Much of the Isle Royale mining had begun before water levels subsided to their present stages, judging from the elevation of the mine shafts. Mining went on for several thousand years, and some of the timbered shafts went deep into the rock. The engineering challenges must have been substantial when one considers that shafts were dug with stone tools, using fire, wooden wedges, and plain persistence to work away the bedrock. It is all the more interesting that fire was used to heat and expand the rock, and water to cool and shrink it—this cracked the rock and made mining possible—but that fire was not used to melt, mold, or cast the ore.

About 165 miles southwest of Voyageurs Park at Lake Itasca is a giant bison-kill site, where hunters ambushed the animals fording Nicollet Creek, dated to about 7,000 B.C. This was during a warming period lasting about 2,000 years when the prairies nearly reached the area. Found there among the bison bones, weapons, and tools was the skeleton of a dog, the earliest known in Minnesota. This apparently was a time when nomadic big-game hunting was no longer the exclusive way of life, and humans became semi-nomadic, hunting small game, caribou, and elk, and gathering fruits and vegetables. Harvesting wild rice and maple sap occurred in succeeding centuries.

Near Nett Lake Village on the Nett Lake Indian Reservation, about 35 miles southeast of the park, ancient petroglyphs are carved in the granite of Spirit Island. The age and origin of these petroglyphs is not known. The village site is thought to be one of the oldest continuously occupied Indian communities in the region.

West of the park about 25 miles on Highway 11 is the Grand Mound, the largest Indian mound in several states and one of the most significant in the country. There the Minnesota Historical Society has erected and staffed a sophisticated interpretative center, one of the finest of its kind. Architecturally the center mirrors the conformation and setting of the mound. The multi-media displays inside spiral the visitor through the millennia of successive civilizations and cultures, much as they are revealed through archaeological research on nearby mounds. The Grand Mound, 50 feet high and 100 feet in diameter, although disturbed at the surface, has not been excavated and will not be. The interpretative center is a half mile away, and only footpaths winding through the groves of tall trees provide access to the mound.

An 1895 survey recorded over 10,000 Indian mounds in Minnesota. Most have disappeared as a result of farming, logging, and road construction. However, even in 1895 Grand Mound stood out. Until not too long ago it was thought that the moundbuilders, the Hopewell, were a mysterious and separate race centered in Ohio and Illinois. Speculative literature in the late 1800s sought to connect the moundbuilders to lost Atlantis, ancient Phoenicia, Egypt, Israel, and elsewhere. More is known now, and the facts are simpler and, in a way, more exciting.

Moundbuilding was widespread and represented a growing cultural and spiritual expression. It was a ceremonial and utilitarian method of interring the dead in primary and secondary burials. Some primary burials were in pits below surface level—knees were flexed, the head rested on the knees in a near-foetal posture. Grave goods of copper, shell ornaments, and tools are found with such burials. In some mounds the pits were covered with logs, and the logs were burned. The mound was then built atop, with secondary burials added later.

Secondary burials were of bodies first put on platforms, in trees, temporarily buried and later exhumed, or dismembered and then buried. The bigger bones were bundled for such burial, and there is evidence that sometimes the marrow and brain were extracted. Because the ground is frozen half the year, secondary burials make sense as does today's north-country practice of placing coffins in vaults for springtime interment.

The Grand Mound is located in a remote spot. It came to be where it is not by accident, but for the soundest of commercial and strategic reasons. This religious and spiritual monument was erected at the mouth of the Big Fork River as it empties into the Rainy. It was a crossroads for travelers from the Mississippi system into the voyageurs highway, and thence east to Lake Superior, west to Winnipeg and on to Hudson Bay and the Northwest Territories, or west and south to the prairies.

An entirely new technology is revolutionizing archaeology, and the next few years may bring an explosion of knowledge. Sparked by space technology made available for civilian use, and some hard-driving, imaginative Park Service archaeologists, the days of pick-and-shovel digging into our past are ending. Photographic techniques convert old black-and-white aerial photographs into color-coded pictures that show soil compaction where ancient fields, roads, and villages once existed; where two, three, or four dwellings were superimposed successively on the ruins of the previous structures, but where nothing is now visible on the ground. We suddenly discover ancient Indian roads, with curbs, leading into Mexico, though we do not yet know what was transported over them; we discover line-of-sight towers 20 miles apart leading from settlement to settlement where signal lights guided travelers and communicated news; we discover commerce and trade in prehistoric times. In the north country, the new technology in the hands of Park Service archaeologists may shove present knowledge into obsolescence, may show the extent of fields and villages in connection with the mounds, and routes of commerce about which we can only guess now. The same technology may enable us to analyze the composition of lake bottoms and swamplands through analysis of aerial photography, instead of laboriously taking core samples, examining pollen content, and then projecting the time, duration, and makeup of flora over the millennia. Archaeologists suspect that early Americans traveled and traded widely, and settled in communities thousands of years ago. The shovel, trowel, and sifting screen will be relegated to the role of confirmation of the time-machine capabilities of our space age.

Archaeologists term the cultures of the period 1000 B.C. to 1700 A.D. the Woodland Tradition. The Grand Mound has given rise to a specific early woodland culture, the Laurel. The name has nothing to do with Indians; it was taken from a post office and store that stood nearby when archaeologists first identified their findings as belonging to a unique culture. Laurel in its various forms covered an area from the park into Ontario, south into the Mississippi watershed, east past Michigan into the Great Lakes area toward upper New York, and west to the Red River of the North. The people of the Laurel Culture, and their successors, the Black-duck Culture, were racially and tribally the same, and are thought by some to be the ancestors of today's Sioux or Dakota Indians.

The broad Woodland Tradition differed from its predecessor the Archaic by developing agriculture, constructing burial mounds, which connote religious ceremonials, and introducing pottery; a life of permanent settlements led to a dramatic population surge, a common phenomenon throughout the world when nomads turned to domestication. In northern Minnesota the staple food was protein-rich wild rice (as against maize, or corn, farther south), augmented by berries, other fruits, vegetables, and maple sugar. The farther south one went, the more one found cultivation of squash and maize; in central and southern Minnesota the maize culture predominated. It is still unclear when the Minnesota Woodland Indians came to use wild rice and maple sugar.

Many kinds of crosscurrents interplayed and intermixed in the Woodland period, and this was reflected in contemporary northern Minnesota life. Hopewell beliefs and practices traveled the rivers north to become incorporated or adapted; northern copper went south. The practice of tempering clay with crushed shell traveled north, replacing the less effective use of grit. Old north-country campsites yield pottery fragments with shell tempering at the top layers, grit-tempered pottery beneath.

This interplay of influences underlines the importance of commercial links and trade routes. The people who carried an idea or a practice from Illinois, Missouri, or Iowa to the Canadian border, or copper the other way (or perhaps conch shells to the north), traveled the rivers. One of the major routes north, going up the Mississippi, took off from the north shore of Lake Winnibigoshish through smaller lakes and rivers to a portage now called Cutfoot Sioux. The ancient route went down the Big Fork River to Rainy River and the Grand Mound. There were other routes, and archaeological maps show Woodland travel courses literally criss-crossing Minnesota, indeed all the Middle West.

The archaeological sites within the park, as well as those of the north country, vividly reveal the evolving life-styles of the early, middle, and late Woodland periods. Between 1000 and 1700 A.D. the corn-beans-squash agriculture of the Mississippian tradition influenced the north very sharply, which is revealed in pottery designs. Largely because of the climate, the northern Indians made a distinctive adaptation. Elsewhere nomadic hunting and fishing life-styles were giving way to stable villages and agriculture. Usually 600 to 800 people lived in one community—surrounded, perhaps, by a palisade—and used bottomlands to grow crops, storing harvests in underground pits. In the north, pits were used to store wild rice, and such caches can still be found; communities were smaller, and seasonal migrations were common from wild-rice campsites in the fall to small winter hunting groups, to the sugarbush (maple groves) at spring breakup time, and summer gardening and berrying. These movements became polarized into summer and winter camps, or villages. It was a pattern adopted by the Ojibway when they intruded from east to west in the early 1700s, ultimately defeating and ousting the woodland Sioux and driving them south and west to join the plains Sioux.

Ojibway, or Chippewa, is a name given the Indians by the French, its original meaning obscure. It may stem from the Indian word for "puckered," since Ojibway moccasins are puckered at the seam where the front instep leather is gathered. William W. Warren, Ojibway himself, historian, and member of the first Minnesota legislature, thought that the puckering could also have referred to the shrinking of human flesh when it was roasted, although this was atypical of Ojibway practices. The Ojibway name for themselves is *Ahnishinabe*, meaning Original People (Warren translates it as Spontaneous People).

Ahnishinabe are members of the Algonquian language family which includes Cree, Passamaquoddy, Penobscot, Delaware, Miami, Illinois, Sauk, Fox, Menominee, Potawatomie, Ottawa, Arapahoe, Cheyenne, Blackfoot, and many others. These are the people who occupied the American woodlands from the eastern seaboard to the prairies, from Hudson's Bay to Texas. The Algonquian language stock has been compared to the role of romance languages in Europe; most of the over 100 Indian words that have passed into American English are Algonquian (e.g., opossum, raccoon, persimmon, hominy, terrapin, squash, moose). Among Algonquian legendary and historical figures are King Philip, Powhatan, Tecumseh, Pontiac, and Pocahontas. Within the Algonquian fold the Ojibway is one of the largest tribes.

The Ojibway migration west began on the east coast around 1000 A.D. its causes shrouded in legend. However, several factors do emerge: enmity with the Iroquis (Six Nations) of upper New York; widespread disease, which Indians believed resulted from sinfulness; a low ebb in the group's spiritual life. The west promised not only solutions to practical problems but also spiritual renewal— mythologically the course of the soul was west, hence the dead were buried facing that direction.

The exact dates are questionable, though Warren estimates that it was in the 1400s that the Ojibway established their new spiritual and central base at LaPointe on Madeline Island. This is the largest of the 20 Apostle Islands in Lake Superior, off the south shore near the thumb of the Bayfield Peninsula. Madeline is 14 miles long and 3 miles wide at its narrows. It offered more security than the mainland. The cliff-shored, hilly Apostles are near the Brule River, a canoe route to the Mississippi via the St. Croix River; they are also close to the mouth of the St. Louis River (the site of Duluth and Superior today, with the community of Fond du Lac a few miles upstream), with its canoe routes to the border lakes and to the Mississippi farther north than the Brule route. The Apostles were also proximate to Isle Royale and the Keweenaw Peninsula copper deposits. The soil and climate of Madeline Island were conducive to agriculture, and Warren reports traces of ancient gardens and even older stumps of very large trees in these plots that grew maize, squash, and other vegetables. At the Apostles the westward migration ran into stiffening resistance from the Woodland Sioux in Minnesota and the Fox in Wisconsin; a major mainland village of the Ojibway at Chequamaugon Bay had to be moved to the island after devastating attacks. The Apostle Islands were designated a National Seashore four months before Voyageurs National Park was so designated.

By the early 1700s the Ojibway were deserting LaPointe and driving inland in earnest. Beachheads had been established and war parties, followed by family groups, fanned out in Minnesota and Canada along the canoe routes to Grand Portage, Nett Lake, Fond du Lac, Mille Lacs, Leech and Cass Lakes. It is an oversimplification to say that this happened because the Ojibway made an alliance with the French fur traders, who were then beginning to move into the area, and obtained guns and trade goods which gave them an advantage. As with all historical developments, several factors played a role. The Woodland Dakotas had been spreading into the prairies, drawn by small groups of Dakotas who had drifted westward and built a life around the migrating buffalo herds, using horses that had been introduced from Mexico by other plains Indians; the eastern Ojibway spread along both sides of the lakes and were feeling the growing pressure of French and later English settlers; also, the fur trade was advantageous and better pursued inland. Once again there was a spiritual malaise and religious upheaval that made LaPointe seem contaminated, and led to a renewed vigor in westward movement and to a reconstitution of Ojibway religious expression, the Midewiwin, the great religious society.

Simultaneously the French fur trade was moving west, graduating from sporadic exploring parties seeking a mythical Northwest Passage to trading parties, then major trading sessions where inland Ojibway brought quantities of furs to Sault St. Marie, Mackinac Island, or even Montreal. Before long the fur trade was organized, and French depots and trading posts were established on Lake Superior and inland, where Indians exchanged furs for blankets, beads, copper and iron tools, kettles, firearms, and alcohol. It was more efficient for all concerned to eliminate the Indians' travel time, and the French hired contract canoeists from among their own immigrants to transport goods and furs between Montreal and the depots. This blossoming of the organized fur trade happened quickly between the 1600s, when the French first saw Lake Superior, and the 1700s, when the posts were springing up.

By then Ojibways had established themselves permanently on the stretch from Grand Portage to Rainy Lake to Winnipeg in alliance with the Cree, Gros Ventres, and Assiniboin to the northwest. Ojibway were at Nett Lake and thence southwestward through the Big Fork River country. Critical battles between Ojibways and Dakota were fought at Kathio (Mille Lacs), Sandy Lake, Crow Wing, Red Lake, Cutfoot Sioux, Cross Lake, St. Croix Falls, and Elk River between 1736 and 1800. The warfare ranged to the prairies, throughout the Mississippi River Valley to the present site of Minneapolis and St. Paul. The Kathio, St. Croix Falls, and Cutfoot Sioux battles were probably definitive.

Cutfoot Sioux in 1736 was fought at the height of the land portage between the Hudson Bay and Mississippi watersheds, where the headwaters of the Big Fork River flow north toward Rainy Lake and the Grand Mound, and the southward rivers feed into lakes rich in wild rice, then to Lake Winnibigoshish and the Mississippi. Anticipating the Ojibway, the Dakota built a sizable mound next to the portage trail, and incised a 12-foot turtle, a war symbol, into the flat top facing northeast, the direction from which the Ojibway would come. The turtle sign failed to deter the Ojibway; in fact, they won the battle. Then they transposed the turtle's head and tail so that it could serve as a warning to the Dakota, should they be inclined to return. The mound, a rare itaglio, is located in the northeast corner of the Chippewa National Forest, preserved by the Forest Service.

Some historical accounts portray this hundred years' war as a chaotic, impulsive series of events, as spur-of-the-moment encounters. It can also be viewed as a classical military envelopment, since the Ojibway sent out two flanking arcs. The southern arc spread down the Brule and St. Croix toward the Twin Cities, the northern flank (and first to be firmly established) moved up the St. Louis River and in from Grand Portage, using its deep woods and riverways base to drive south. This is what lent the Cutfoot Sioux battle its importance, just as Red Lake opened the avenue to the prairies and safeguarded Winnipeg for the Ojibway and their allies. Caught in the middle of the two pincers were the rich forest, lake lands, and rice fields of the upper Mississippi and the avenues to the present North and South Dakota. The final battles took place in this midland.

Through the years and generations of the war, the Ojibway maintained and even strengthened their dodaimic, or clan, structure. The dodaims, named for animals such as bear, marten, loon, and crane, numbered more than 20, and were inherited from the father's side. Marriage within a dodaim was forbidden as virtually incestuous, and marriage outside the tribe but to a different dodaim was accepted though not frequent. The dodaims had complex, unique traditions and relationships. The French learned to respect these and to use them—observing the fine points of whom to deal with on a particular subject and in what order of eminence. It could not have been too different from Bourbon court etiquette and the jealousy of French aristocrats. Nor were dodaimic politics less treacherous than politics in any other society bound by clan, religion, and long tradition.

The Ojibway religion was handed down in elaborate initiation rites which were recorded in pictographs on birchbark scrolls. The Midewinin moral structure, taught in progressive steps to those male members of the tribe who wished to join, urged the doing of good for its own sake, social responsibility, and sharing. One religious practice, taught from early youth, encouraged boys to learn to fast for gradually longer periods of time as an exercise in self-discipline, as a survival skill, and ultimately as an inducement to visions and dreams that would help to guide one's life.

The Ojibway life-style in the woodlands did not differ too much from that of the Dakota whom they replaced, or in its essentials from that of the Woodland Indians from whom it derived. It was a seasonal life cycle nourished by the richness of the land as well as by its beauty.

Early spring sun set the maple sap to rising, while night frosts drove it to the roots again. This was the time to move from scattered winter camps to a seasonally used, semipermanent camp in the sugarbush. Since this occasioned a gathering of people, it was an annual social as well as economic event. Birch and other trees were occasionally tapped for sugar sap, but maple contained more sugar. The framework for the lodges was usually left standing from year to year, and food was cached in deep pits. This food was sometimes preserved in *makuks*, birchbark containers sewed together and then gummed at the seams with pine pitch. Makuks contained wild rice, which, if kept dry, could last many years, or that staple pemmican, which was dried meat and dried berries mixed with fat. The sugarcamp also contained stores of hundreds of small birchbark containers used to collect sap, and the other paraphernalia necessary for collecting and boiling down sap to make sugar.

Sugartime lasted up to two months, during which canoes were built because birchbark was at its strongest and travel was restricted by the breakup of lake ice. In the warming days the ice became rotten and unsafe, but the water was not yet open and running. When the sap stopped running and the lakes were open, families moved to the summer village and a life of gardening, fishing, and eventually late July and August berry picking. Berries were stored dried, either alone or in pemmican.

The wild-rice harvest began in late August and lasted well into September, or later in some years. It played the economic and nutritional role that maize did farther south, though wild rice is richer in protein. It grows wild in the rivers and lakes, and is harvested by bending the tall, reedy stalks of this undomesticated wild oat over a canoe, then rapping them with a stick so that the ripe grains shatter into the bottom. Sometimes families returned to the same rice bed annually. Clumps of stalks were tied together at the top— the particular knot designating which family would return to harvest—to hold in ripening grains until most were ready to reap, since the grains ripen at different times. Once garnered, the grains were parched, then threshed by jigging on them.

Fishing and hunting were done all year, any surplus meat smoked or dried for storage. Principal food sources were lake sturgeon, walleye and northern pike, whitefish, caribou, elk, moose, and, to a lesser extent, white-tailed deer. Deer were more of a grassland and borderland forest animal, driven into the woods by farming. In the winter rabbits, partridge, and small game were snared; beaver, muskrat, and porcupine furnished food. When buffalo were within hunting range, parties would travel to the prairies to hunt, a trip of a few days. Ducks, geese, and passenger pigeons were plentiful during the open-water months.

By late fall villages would scatter to set up winter quarters; crowding was not conducive to winter hunting. If the food supply permitted, surpluses were cached at the sugarbush for the following spring.

This life was not the bare-bones struggle for subsistence and survival that is sometimes depicted. The work *was* hard: boiling down maple sap took much firewood and long hours of fire-tending; the winds came up and the weather turned cold just as the wild rice was ripening to a fine point; a snowstorm followed by deep cold hit just as firewood ran low, and the meat supply was down because unexpected company stayed a bit too long. The rules of hospitality and sharing were rigid, need breeding a moral value. The Ojibway life had many games and contests for young and old: snowsnake, sleight of hand challenges to manual dexterity, guessing and gambling games, many kinds of sports such as lacrosse. And except in summer, telling legends, stories, and myths, the second most important method of instruction and education: the first was by example of parents and elders.

An important account of Ojibway life in the late 1700s and early 1800s was written by John Tanner. As a boy he had been kidnapped near his southern Ohio home and taken north to be raised by Great Lakes Ojibway in place of an Indian child who had died. Tanner grew to adulthood, married, and raised a family as an Ojibway in the border-lakes area. He lived in the Rainy Lake area for several years, wintered in the park, and traveled often between Grand Portage and Hudson's Bay, trapping and hunting; some of his trips took him to Sault St. Marie and Mackinac. Tanner's *Narrative* makes fascinating, but sometimes difficult, reading: he unreels it in Indian fashion, assuming that the reader will know the places and distances, and that the reader can somehow put the chronology and relationships of events and people in order. The account is unique, and closely read, it is heartrending. Tanner in his matter-of-fact style, in his prosaic way, tells of the destruction of the Ojibway as a functioning civil body and nation. This was brought about only in small part by the fur trade, which replaced seasonal harmony with commerce, trade, and a barter or money economy. More devastating was the replacement of French rule by British in 1763, even though the contract voyageurs who manned the trade canoes were still French.

The French had not been saints. They had no compunction about introducing alcohol as a staple of the trade, or of spreading disease, or of playing one tribe off against another. But, essentially the French accepted and respected the Ojibway as they were, dealt with the tribal structures and with the leaders that the Indians had chosen. They made an effort to learn the Indian language and to use it.

This was not due to the innate goodness of the French; simply, their primary aim was to find the Northwest Passage and to get rich on the fur trade. Fortune hunters are not interested in land titles. But the English prized territoriality and ownership, as did the Americans, even more after 1812. Their regimes alienated the land and exploited its riches.

The English and Americans tended to dominate and to acquire land. They dealt with Ojibway leaders whom *they* selected and designated, disregarding the dodaimic structure and hereditary, religious, spiritual, and social relationships. It was then that being Indian meant being second-rate, that starvation and degradation became frequent, and that the people who had voyaged throughout the area and lived in concert with it became its prisoners.

Tanner tells of beaver becoming scarce because of overtrapping, and then coming close to extinction owing to an epidemic of distemper. He casually mentions the fervent religious movement, centered on a prophet, that swept maniacally through Ojibway and other tribes, as they sought relief in fantasy when no practical solutions were at hand.

There would come times when Indians were persuaded or forced to accept delimited territories as their own; these were further shrunk to reservations; in turn the reservations were parceled out among Indians "in their best interest" and "in order to civilize them" for homesteading and farming, while their "surplus" reservation lands were auctioned off, given away, or taken by the government. The beginning of this chain of events was concurrent with the fur trade, if not caused by it.

4

Voyageurs of the Fur Trade

Furs in medieval Europe were a badge of rank and office, considered luxuries, and regulated by laws of kings and church. Only those of royal blood were allowed to wear certain furs; monks and others low in the hierarchy were forbidden furs, and only higher ecclesiastics could wear them. Sumptuary laws (laws controlling the allotment of luxuries by social class), particularly those of England from 1300 to 1600, reserved ermine, sable, marten, and genet to the royal family; lesser furs could be worn by the middle class, the poor wore rabbit, lamb, and cat. These laws were not always strictly enforced, but since furs were expensive, cost tended to restrict their use.

Romans, Greeks, and Chinese valued furs and tried to regulate their use. Practices relating value and rarity of furs to social ranking go back 3500 years. By the end of the Middle Ages, European sources of fur were shrinking; northern and central Europe was trapped out, and demand, coupled with European discovery of

North America, created an industry and a wealth, as well as a fashion, that broke down the sumptuary laws until furs were worn by all who could afford them. Some nations were quicker than others to realize the potential of the fur trade; the Spanish sought gold and converts, the English commerce and colonies, the French coupled search for the Northwest Passage and precious metals with fur before the pilgrims landed at Plymouth Rock. English colonists were huddled in eastern seaboard enclaves, a hundred years from crossing the Alleghenies, when the French were trading furs from Lake Superior, tapping the riches from the midcontinent to the prairies and Hudson Bay, and shipping them east over the Great Lakes to Montreal, Quebec, and Paris.

French, English, Spanish, and Portuguese fishermen had been catching cod off Newfoundland in annual trips from 1500 on, following Cabot's trip to Canada in-the 1490s. In 1536, Cartier pushed up the St. Lawrence River to the site of today's Montreal and the Lachine Rapids (near Montreal International Airport), and then attempted, unsuccessfully, to establish a settlement at Quebec. Champlain finally succeeded in 1608, but by then Frenchmen had been swapping furs for hatchets, knives, and other goods in the Gulf of St. Lawrence area. Champlain built a trading post at Montreal in 1611 and traveled inland at least as far as Lake Huron. There are indications that he knew of Lake Superior, and that Indians from at least that far, if not farther, west were bringing furs to Montreal, or trading them to intermediary tribes to be relayed. By 1618-20 Brule was in Lake Superior and not necessarily the first Frenchman there.

The French practice of issuing licenses and monopolies was at odds with their attempt to bring in settlers. The profit was in the fur trade, and monopolies held that profit to a very few. The alternative was unlicensed fur trading, which probably resulted in bribery and kickbacks by unlicensed traders, since somewhere along the commercial or mercantile chain the furs had to be legitimized.

Richelieu, master of France, participated in forming the Company of One Hundred Associates in 1628, which had a monopoly on the fur trade in return for a commitment to bring settlers to New France. The trade was interrupted by a naval war with England and temporary British capture of Quebec. There were further interruptions through repeated wars with the Iroquois. Under Champlain, the French had allied themselves with the Algonquians against the Iroquois. The Iroquois, from their strong base in upstate New York, raided Indian fur-trading parties on their way to Montreal and Quebec. After 1650 and Iroquois victories over the Hurons, reputedly the merchants and middlemen among the Algonquians, the bulk of the Algonquians were driven west of Lake Huron to Lake Michigan. From then on, with some exceptions, the French took the trade to the Indians and brought back the furs.

A new breed came into being, the *coureurs de bois*, or woods rangers, who traveled inland over the rivers and lakes, using the Indians' birchbark canoes. Some of the *coureurs de bois* traded on their own, being gone for one to three years at a time and learning to live in the woods as the Indians did. Occasionally, if a trading trip had been very successful, the *coureur* would hire Indians to ferry the bales of furs to Montreal with him on the return trip, and a flotilla would round the point at St. Anne's—where a church would later be built—go around the rapids of Lachine, and up to the wharf at the village of Montreal. By 1641 there was a mission at Sault St. Marie where Lake Superior spills into Lake Huron; Nicollet, dressed in a damask robe and brandishing pistols, had claimed the interior for France in ceremonies at Green Bay, surely knowing he was nowhere near the Orient despite his Chinese style of dress; and in 1654 Médard Chouart, Sieur des Groseilliers, returned from a trading trip with 50 fur-laden Indian canoes, to a rousing reception at Quebec.

Groseilliers' next trip in 1659-60 was not licensed. He was accompanied by his young brother-in-law, Pierre Esprit Radisson, and they passed Mackinac Island near the junction of Lakes Huron, Michigan, and Superior. Instead of turning south into Lake Michigan as they had inidcated they would, they went west into Lake Superior and then inland by way of Grand Portage into Rainy Lake where they wintered. On their return to Montreal, the governor confiscated their furs, and Groseilliers and Radisson were outraged. They were so embittered by what seemed to them piracy,

by the restrictiveness of the French licensing and monopoly practices, and most of all by the obstinacy of the French government
in not understanding the commercial realities and potential of the
north country, that they took a drastic and historic step. They
went to England, ultimately persuaded the British of the value of
the interior north, and succeeded when the Hudson's Bay Company was formed. Hudson's Bay was to develop a fur trade from
James Bay and the Hayes River, near the Nelson estuary. The company did well at first, drawing from the local Indians and then
those farther away toward Lake Winnipeg. But the French had
been there too long and were too well established. They interdict-
ed the fledgling company's routes and suppliers, and ultimately
captured the trading posts on Hudson Bay.

In the course of their lobbying efforts in England, Radisson
wrote a book about the wonders, beauties, and riches of interior
America. The book told such a fabulous tale of exotic lands and
people that it became the equivalent of today's sensational best-
seller. It was highly inaccurate and exaggerated Radisson's adven-
tures and his role; among other liberties he took, Radisson wrote
himself into his brother-in-law's first journey. Radisson's book became one of a genre. In later years Father Hennepin, Jonathan
Carver, and a host of others wrote about canoe travel, Indians, and
the American interior, and this literature may have had more to do
with exciting European curiosity and greed than did the actual fur-
trade profits. In recent times the literary traditions of the region
and the role of regional books in arousing public interest and sym-
pathy are represented by the writings of Sigurd Olson, Florence
and Lee Jaques, Grace Lee Nute, Arnold Bolz, and others.

While the initial Hudson's Bay Company venture faltered, the
French expanded rapidly. Missions sprang up on Madeline Island,
erstwhile "heart" of the Ojibway, and elsewhere. Explorers/
traders were sent out with sizable parties: Joliet to the Mississippi
by way of Lake Michigan, the Fox and Wisconsin Rivers; Duluth
through central Minnesota to Mille Lacs, as much the home base
of Woodland Sioux as Madeline Island had been to the Ojibway.
French installations were going up at Kaministiquia (later Ft.
William/Port Arthur, today Thunder Bay, Ontario), and Nipigon

on Lake Superior; at the St. Croix River above its juncture with the Mississippi. Unsanctioned and unlicensed French traders operated even more widely.

Although the French court in Paris could not control private traders, they could and did exact a toll for every license application. After a meeting of 200 traders in Montreal on August 17, 1692, Pierre Charles LeSueur opened a post on Madeline, then another at the mouth of the St. Croix, and finally applied for a 10-year-monopoly in furs and minerals on the Upper Mississippi, going north from the St. Croix juncture. Paris finally granted the monopoly application on condition that LeSueur go *up* the Mississippi from its mouth, exploring as he went, and bolstering France's claim to the territory. The ensuing grueling trip required two years. One of the officers with LeSueur, d'Iberville, left the party and founded what is now Biloxi, Mississippi, in 1699. By 1700 LeSueur was past St. Anthony's Falls (Minneapolis-St. Paul) and had built a trading post on the Minnesota River at Blue Earth. Named Ft. L'Hullier, it was in the middle of LeSueur's duly licensed monopoly area; no sooner was it erected than seven *coureurs de bois* showed up, caught in their fur-trading enterprises by oncoming winter. They stayed at Ft. L'Huillier until spring and helped kill about 400 buffalo. Presumably much of the meat was manufactured into pemmican and packaged, a staple food of the fur trade. In later years pemmican factories came into existence along the prairies where buffalo hunters slaughtered hundreds of animals, Indians were hired to strip and dry the meat, then pound it, mix it with dried berries and fat, and package it for the fur trade. The pemmican bales were transported over the rivers and the voyageurs highway to principal depots such as Rainy Lake, Grand Portage, and Madeline.

Although England regained Hudson's Bay under the Treaty of Utrecht as France kept losing on the seas and in Europe and paid off with American assets, French dominance was cresting. Canadian-born Pierre Gaultier de Varennes, Sieur de la Verendrye, was stationed at the Nipigon post in 1727 when a local Ojibway, Auchagah, drew a map for him showing a chain of rivers and lakes leading to salt water. The quest for a Northwest Passage had motivated much early exploration and was good stock in trade for license applications in European courts. Verendrye asked for 100 men, money, and supplies, to look anew. He received the license on condition that he seek the Northwest Passage to China, and set off in 1731 with three of his four sons, 50 soldiers and voyageurs. Although voyageur means traveler in French, in Canada it came to denote a northwoodsman and canoeist in someone's employ, as against the *coureur de bois* who worked for himself.

The party left Montreal in June and arrived at Grand Portage August 26. One son and a nephew were sent inland and wintered on Rainy Lake where they built Ft. St. Pierre; the remainder of the party traveled up the Superior north shore to Kaministiquia for the winter. The next spring the main party joined the Rainy Lake vanguard and they all went on to Lake of the Woods where Ft. Charles was erected. This establishment was palisaded 100 feet by 60, with 15-foot-high walls sunk 3 feet in the ground, a watchtower, two gates, four buildings, a magazine, storehouse, chapel, and two cabins. The Northwest Passage was not being sought very rapidly, but the forts and trading posts were being built briskly. Perhaps Verendrye knew, as others had before him, that there were waterway connections to Hudson Bay, which is salt water. Verendrye's nephew Jeremaye took the traded furs back to Montreal after spring breakup in 1733 and returned by August. Far from being isolated, the Verendrye posts had much company, some of whom had to be ceremoniously greeted, given gifts, and bid adieu in style. Among the visitors in 1733 was a Sioux party of 300 on the way to attack Ojibway at Madeline; another Sioux party of 500 on the way to attack Plains Sioux; Cree, Assiniboin, and Ojibway visitors; and 150 Indian canoes bringing pemmican, wild rice, and other food to the post. Verendrye's men planted corn, peas, and also gathered rice.

Verendrye did pursue his explorations, going past the Missouri to the Rockies in 1742-43, building more posts and forts at Winnipeg, on the Assiniboine and Saskatchewan rivers. There is uncertainty about how far west and north the Verendrye party reached beyond their plaque found in the Dakotas and their trading posts.

They suffered from the violence that plagued the fur trade throughout its existence. Verendrye traded with Ojibway and Sioux. He tried repeatedly to arrange peace treaties between the two tribes because warfare interfered with Indian fur trapping; it also posed a danger to his men. In 1736 a war party of Sioux killed 21 of Verendrye's men, including one of his sons, on an island in Lake of the Woods. Another son, Joseph, was involved in a prolonged and sometimes vicious rivalry with another French trader, Marin.

With the Verendryes, their forts and trading posts, their gardens and husbandry, their willingness to do business with everyone, one senses a maturing of the fur trade into a more solid institution. The trade had been ongoing for about 140 years, conducted by licensees and freebooters. But the time of the *coureur de bois* was coming to a close, and voyageurs were manning canoes, employed by the more successful traders, while Indians were encouraged to trap. The Verendryes were Canadians, even though their ties to France were strong and the elder Verendrye had traveled to France as a young man to fight for king and country. The French-Canadian population, centered around Montreal and Quebec, was growing and some were by now third and fourth generation, whose fathers and grandfathers had spent years in the backcountry as *coureurs de bois* or, later, as voyageurs. Montreal, a village of 2,300 in the 1640s, was several times more populous now; the population of New France was 55,000 in 1754. The villages and farms provided manpower for the ranks of the voyageurs.

The Verendryes' license was revoked in 1744, but their system of forts and posts continued to draw a vigorous trade; the merchant towns of New France prospered despite the renewed European war between France and England. In 1756 this war spilled into North America, focusing on conflict over the Ohio Valley fur trade. France lost Canada in the treaty of 1763, and English officials and traders lost no time. Within a year they announced there would be no more monopolies and licenses would be issued to several traders for any area. This set the stage for cutthroat competition and armed conflict between the Montreal traders and those of the Hudson's Bay Company.

The English convoked a conference of Ojibway at Niagara in 1764 seeking to cement relationships. This was not easy because for over 150 years, the French-Ojibway alliance had worked well for both sides and there had been considerable intermarriage between *coureurs de bois*, and later voyageurs, and Ojibway. A new population of buffalo hunters and voyageurs of mixed blood was coming into being, the *metis* of the lake country, particularly around Lake Winnipeg.

British traders like Alexander Henry flooded the area, hiring French-Canadian voyageurs to man their canoes and clerk at their posts. Henry had narrowly escaped when the Ojibway, true to their alliance with the French, attacked and sacked the strategic British-occupied fort at Mackinac in 1763, the last year of the war. Henry had been hidden in the upstairs loft when the Ojibway lured the garrison outside to watch a vigorous lacrosse game, then attacked and killed most of them. The Mackinac fort has been painstakingly and accurately reconstructed, and stands in sight of Mackinac Bridge which today spans the straits, connecting upper and lower Michigan. Two years after the Ojibway attack on Mackinac, in 1765, Henry was back as a trader, setting up at nearby Sault St. Marie and farther into the Lake Superior country at Chequamaugon Bay near today's Ashland, Wisconsin. Fur traders, Indians, and explorers alike had always recognized Mackinac, and particularly Mackinac Island, as a principal, strategic location in the Great Lakes, since it controlled traffic among three of the lakes. Mackinac is a shortening of the Indian word *michilimackinac*, or turtle, an appropriate name for the island not only because of its shape, but also because, as indicated earlier, the turtle was a war symbol for some tribes.

Shortly after Henry returned to Mackinac and the Lake Superior country, trader John Askin began constructing a major depot at Grand Portage. Fur-trade construction was efficient and quick, aided by the abundance of good timber. Logs were squared with a regular ax, since broadaxes were scarce and traders complained that even if one was procured, the French-Canadian voyageurs would not know how to use it. Squared logs were morticed or grooved for sawed window and door frames. Squared beams were used to cap the rectangular walls, then rafters and a ridge pole (spelled *rige* by some contemporary journal keepers) formed the roof. Roofing was thatched straw or, more often, slabs of white-cedar bark. A stone fireplace and chimney, clay caulking, and oiled parchment for windows completed the exterior. Inside, the floor was sometimes planked, floor boards converted the loft into separate rooms. It required about a month's work to build Ft. Charles, for example, but Grand Portage was unlike any of the other posts before or since.

The portage had long been used as a principal entry point to the interior, and many French traders had convoyed their goods and camped there, finding, as had the Indians before them, that it *was* the best funnel to the interior, despite the hilly, rocky, and in places swampy nine-mile trail. Grand Portage is sheltered on a lovely bay flanked by two small mountains; in the center of the bay and offshore half a mile is an island that protects the harbor from wind, waves, and Lake Superior currents. The beach is clean and gravelly, and the setting among the most beautiful in the north country. Here a large compound arose, eventually including a great hall for annual meetings of major fur traders and for feeding 100 persons or more at a time. The more successful traders and partnerships banded together in 1779 to form the North West Company—the age of the voyaguers had arrived.

Birchbark *canots de maitre* measuring 35 to 40 feet, or Montreal canoes, hauled trade goods to Grand Portage. Voyageurs using narrow, red-painted paddles signed up for a year or longer to make the trip through the Great Lakes, carry the baled goods over the portage, and return to Montreal by fall. Patronizingly called *mangers du lard*, or porkeaters, by the more experienced men who wintered and traded in the interior, the younger men were drawn from the farms and villages of the east. The staple diet for *mangers du lard* was bacon and corn or dried peas.

The voyageurs tended to be short and stocky, generally with short legs and broad chests. One tall man among the rest made for awkward canoe-carrying and paddling. A premium was paid the *chanseur* who led the singing en route, helping to pace the 40-to-60-strokes-a-minute rhythm of the paddles. Premiums were also paid the *avant* (bowman) and the *gouvernail* (steersman); the rest, the *milieux*, paddled, sang, and portaged. From the ranks of the *mangers du lard* the stronger, more resilient men were chosen for work in the interior.

Customarily the Montreal brigades left in May, as soon after spring breakup as possible. In winter the inventory and resupplying were completed; the process of placing orders from the farflung posts, collating them in Montreal, forwarding them to London, and receiving the shipment for distribution often took three years. A crew of 12 paddled a Montreal *canot de maitre*, carrying up to 4,000 pounds of cargo. Cedar paddles measured 3½ feet for *milieux*, about 4 feet and wider for *gouvernail*, and even longer and wider for the *avant* who guided through rapids and around obstacles, although the *gouvernail* ordinarily steered. Montreal canoes stopped at St. Anne's Church of the Voyageurs for prayers and blessings, not only because of the hazardous trip, but also for those who would sign up for duty in the interior once they arrived at Grand Portage six weeks later, and who would not be home again for several years.

Once at Grand Portage, the Montrealers would unload and carry goods to the north end where a smaller depot, Ft. Charlotte, was constructed. On the return hike, fur bales were sometimes brought back, but rarely canoes. The *hivernauts*, or winterers, used smaller 25-foot *canots du nord*, which were kept at the Ft. Charlotte end. These canoes had crews of eight to ten and a freight capacity of 2,000 to 3,000 pounds.

Canoes were purchased from the Indians or made in yards by Indian employees. Birchbark was fastened to a cedar frame with *watape*, spruce roots soaked in water, and sealed with spruce gum; no nails were used. Spare gum, *watape*, and birchbark were carried for repairs. The canoes were so light and maneuverable, yet durable, that old-timers have described riding in one as "floating on a lily pad."

The annual rendezvous at Grand Portage lasted about a month, after which the porkeaters returned to Montreal with the furs. Sometimes *hivernauts* whose terms had ended would join them, and porkeaters who had passed muster would head for the interior. The Montreal canoes arrived home shortly before freezeup, loaded with fur bales. For the *hivernauts* it was a different story.

The trading area had expanded far into the northwest to the Mackenzie River (1789) and the Peace River (1792), when Alexander Mackenzie crossed the Rockies for a view of the Pacific. Cartographer David Thompson, employed by the North West Company to carefully map the area, noted fur packs from Great Slave

Lake at one of the portages he crossed in 1797. Although Grand Portage was halfway between Montreal and the farther outposts, travel was slower in the interior because of the many portages. The trip inland often became a race against winter freezeup. When this happened, brigades destined for Athabasca or more distant locations had to cache their canoes and proceed on foot or by dogsled. During travel in the interior the same pace prevailed as in Great Lakes travel, a tempo of 40 to 60 paddle strokes a minute save in choppy waters, when the pace was quickened; there were hourly "pipes," rests for a few puffs on small clay pipes, and on portages, "poses," regular rest intervals. But the rule was an 18-hour-day.

Once at the post, voyageurs worked under the company clerk, or *comis*. They might trade, do some trapping of their own, hunt for food, or help construct a building during the six months before they could set out again for the rendezvous at Grand Portage. Or they could fight. The rivalry among traders, and particularly between Hudson's Bay and North West, was bloody. Hudson's Bay built a post on Rainy Lake in 1793 and was forced out by 1798; it sent mercenary troops, including some Swiss, back to Rainy Lake in 1816, ousted North West, and rebuilt in 1818. In 1797 some of the North West partners split off and formed the rival X Y Company, both operating out of Grand Portage for several years. Ultimately X Y and North West recombined, and in 1821 Hudson's Bay absorbed North West, but the years in between were marked by raids and counter-raids, bushwhacking, fur thefts, and killings. Life for the winterers differed radically from that of the *mangers du lard*, even though the trading posts drew Indian families who camped nearby while the trapping season was on, and little communities developed around the posts.

The porkeaters were far from the strife and hardship for the six winter months. Their annual trip, beginning at Montreal or Lachine, took them up the Ottawa River, then upstream on the Mattawa to Lake Nipissing; from there it was downstream to Lake Huron and a restocking of food and supplies at Mackinac. Although it was a short paddle to Sault St. Marie, the portage there was long, and Lake Superior loomed ahead. The normal route was along the north shore, past the cliffs, islands, and bays to Grand Portage.

Many small, white crosses made of wood marked places where voyageurs had died. Some were grave markers, others memorials, as in Europe's mountain regions where crosses mark locations where climbers have fallen to their death. The trails of the *hivernauts* in the interior were studded with such death markers where men drowned, were killed, or succumbed to disease. Yet they kept coming, former engagees having seniority in the rehiring, new recruits being scoured from the land. Part of the contract pay was handed over when the men signed on, the balance when their term ended.

Voyageur dress was practical, a mix of wool shirts and caps, deerskin leggings and moccasins. A sash was tied around the waist to gather in the shirt, and *hivernauts* wore a feather or plume, stuck in caps or headbands. The class consciousness distinguishing the *hivernauts* from the *mangers du lard* was enhanced by initiation ceremonies for new *hivernauts* when they crossed the height of land beyond Grand Portage and entered the watershed where all flows were eventually emptied to the north. Initiates took an oath, were sprinkled with a few baptismal drops of water from a wet cedar bough, and in return were expected to treat companions from their portion of liquor. Visiting dignitaries were similarly invested, some of them suspecting it was done more for the treat of drinks than for any other reason. Another ceremony, with utilitarian origins, consisted of marking lob pines or Maypoles at prominent places or heights. A man would climb a tall pine, lop off branches below the crown for about a third of the tree's height, so that it would be noticeable from a distance as a marker. Visiting officials who had lob pines marked in their honor were expected to stand a round of drinks; during the years when the trade was vigorous there were said to be many more lob pines than was really necessary, some of these pines surviving into the twentieth century.

From earliest trading times, liquor figured prominently in the manifests, and was cited in missionaries' complaints as a corrupting influence on voyageurs and Indians. At rendezvous times the voyageurs' brawls were proverbial, and it was a deliberate practice and policy of the trade to foster alcohol consumption and dependency among Indians, exchanging alcohol for furs, food, canoes, and labor. Even the traders who decried the use and the results of liquor continued to trade in it, and it was a staple item along with hatchets, knives, chisels, kettles, pots, beads, and blankets. Ice chisels and knives had become a necessity for beaver trapping, a tool of the trade, and had to be purchased or bartered by the Indians at the beginning of the season if they expected to bring in pelts during the winter and early spring. This evolved into a credit system, with the Indian in debt at the beginning of trapping, hoping to come out ahead at the end, but sometimes working for the same trading post year after year without ever being in the clear. The mounting pressure to catch up came to interfere and ultimately to eliminate the traditional seasonal Indian activities essential to a balanced life and diet, the maple-sugar harvest, the stocking of provisions, the cycle and pattern of wholesome living.

A typical lading for a *canot du nord*, this one leaving Grand Portage for the Red River country in July 1800, consisted of 5 bales merchandise, 1 bale tobacco, 1 bale kettles, 1 case guns, 1 case iron works, 2 rolls twist tobacco, 2 kegs gunpowder, and 10 kegs high wine each containing 9 gallons. Annual licensing figures, probably less than complete, showed that in a representative year 67 licenses were issued for 163 canoes and 163 *bateaux*, 2,139 men, 56,324 gallons rum, 66,207 pounds powder, 899½ hundredweight ball and shot, plus other goods.

There was inevitable loss of goods en route, but the fur-trade profits were enormous. Alexander Henry, the younger, set out for the Red River country from Grand Portage with several canoes loaded with sugar, flour, tobacco, knives, tools, guns, gunpowder, cloth, mirrors, and 10 kegs of liquor in each canoe. He opened for business in the fall, and in one typical year (he stayed eight) sent back pelts or hides of 1,621 beaver, 125 black bear, 49 brown bear, 4 grizzly bear, 862 wolf, 509 fox, 152 raccoon, 322 fisher, 214 otter, 1,456 marten, 507 mink, 45 wolverine, 469 moose, and 12,470 muskrat. Gross sales value, and net profit after costs, made direct and overhead costs about 20 percent.

Another young trader destined for great success and wealth in later life, Peter Pond, made $20,000 in one year and apparently did not consider this particularly noteworthy. Henry Sibley, one of Minnesota's founding fathers, started out as a young trader and in a small partnership did $60,000 worth of business one year. For

Sibley as for others, muskrat were the main cash crop during this phase of the fur trade, and that year the major items were: 389,388 muskrat ($44,702), 1,027 otter ($4,135), 1,139 buffalo robes ($4,156), 3,243 deerskins, probably caribou ($972), 225 beaver ($900), 609 fisher ($913), 2,330 mink ($698), 2,011 raccoon ($603).

In this barter economy the rates of exchange varied from one time and locality to another, but they were always weighted in favor of the trader and against the trapper. A kettle or blanket worth $3 was traded for 60 muskrat skins worth $12, and in other exchanges, beads worth pennies against pelts worth dollars were commonplace. As in today's consumption economy, Indian trappers were encouraged to draw guns, ammunition, tools, blankets, and other goods on credit against which they pledged future furs. A trader's success depended in large part on knowing who was a good credit risk and who was not, and this contributed to their encouraging Indians to do business regularly and to settle in the general area of the post.

Grand Portage today looks much as it did in its heyday as a fur-trade center, thanks in large part to the Grand Portage Ojibway, on whose reservation it is located, who have fought steadfastly against exploitation and despoiling of a place that has great historic and scenic value. Grand Portage Indians today own a modern motel, but were careful that it was unobtrusively placed and built so as not to damage the environment. They have maintained a careful relationship with the Park Service, which operates the reconstructed fort and trading post and maintains the portage trail; and they have successfully fought for locating the main highway, U.S. Route 61 which extends from Interstate 35, so that it will not interfere with the ancient community and will have a scenic view of the lake. As a consequence, today's visitor can walk about the rendezvous grounds and see it as it was 200 years ago. Then the *canots de maitre*, having stopped just short of the bay for the men to freshen up, rounded *Pointe au Chapeaux*, singing in unison, while the *comis* and others on shore would line up at the L-shaped wharf to cheer.

At the peak of the fur trade there were scores of Montreal canoes flipped over on the shore east of the little creek, where porkeaters camped and slept in their shelters. Across the creek the *hivernauts* were camped in tents, their canoes left behind at Ft. Charlotte. The North West Company partners, or *bourgeois*, and their *comis* were housed inside the palisaded compound to transact the business of the year. When the firm functioned well it was divided into several departments, or areas. For example, trade around the Brule and St. Croix Rivers was run from LaPointe on Madeline Island, where the Cadottes and later the Warrens operated the post. Trade on the Upper Mississippi, including Leech and Cass Lakes and, for a time, Red Lake, and down the Mississippi to Crow Wing below Brainerd, was operated from the Fond du Lac Department. Annual discussions about departmental boundaries and who would trade at which locations kept the North Westers reasonably amicable. Not all trading deals were in furs; one year young John B. Cadotte, on a spree in Montreal, borrowed money from trader Alexander Henry, who sold the debt to Alexander Mackenzie. Cadotte eventually had to go to work for Mackenzie in the latter's northern department of North West to work it off.

Hundreds of people gathered at Grand Portage for about a month. The *bourgeois* tried to hold the *hivernauts'* turnaround time to a fortnight to forestall their being caught short on the trail, and also to reduce the mayhem of a longer visit. There were fights and brawls, and a jailhouse had to be built for uncontrollable revelers. The fortnight usually lasted four weeks as several hundred porkeaters mingled with an equal number from the interior, plus clerks and partners, and well over a thousand Ojibway. Summer was as traditional a time for festivities for the Ojibway as it was for the men of the fur trade, a time for dances and ceremonials. The little cornucopia of Grand Portage resonated. Then the Montreal canoes left with the year's take of furs, the *hivernauts* and their *comis* took a last hike over the portage trail to Ft. Charlotte, and some of the Indians scattered to their areas. It was a sudden and dramatic change. No more banquets, saturnalias, or roistering until next year. No more politicking and maneuvering over territories and personnel. No more drums and chanting until the seasons rolled around again.

A vivid eyewitness account of the Grand Portage rendezvous was written by Washington Irving, who described the formal councils of the *bourgeois* and the Montreal agents dressed in silks, banquet menus that included a variety of game, fresh-lake fish, buffalo tongues and beaver tails, and much wine. "While the chiefs thus reveld in hall, and made the rafters resound with bursts of loyalty and old Scottish songs . . . their merriment was echoed by a mongrel legion of retainers, Canadian voyageurs, half breeds, Indian hunters, and vagabond hangers on, who feasted sumptuously (outside) . . . with Old French ditties."

Daniel Harmon, a North West *comis* in 1800, described a dance that followed a rendezvous banquet in the Great Hall. "For musick we had the bag pipe, the violin and the flute. . . . There was a number of ladies of this country; and I was surprised to find that they could conduct with so much propriety, and dance so well."

Inside the celebrants wore Montreal finery, save some department heads and traders from the field in buckskins. Outside it was leggings, breechcloths, wool or buckskin shirts, sashes, and red caps. Indian dress was largely caribou hide, commonly referred to as deerskin, decorated in floral design beading embroidered with trade beads or dyed porcupine quills.

Elsewhere in the world the American Revolution was fought, though there was little sign of it in fur-trade country save the presence of 12 British soldiers at Grand Portage. On paper the treaty ending the war gave much of the territory to the new United States. However, it was unclear just where the dividing line would be drawn. On paper also one of the original 13 states, Virginia, laid claim to the territory. Since few Americans were anywhere near, it was business as usual for the British, and would be for many years to come.

To be on the safe side, the British moved their operations from Grand Portage to Kaministiquia, using young Cadotte to persuade the Indians to go along with the move. Cadotte must have had unusual powers of persuasion, for a few years later when a pan-Indian religious movement swept across the country in the beginnings of a holy war against the whites, Cadotte persuaded a war party of several hundred Ojibway to quit the crusade and turn back. The pan-Indian movement led by Tecumseh and his brother, a prophet, precipitated Indian revolts through much of the country at the same time that the War of 1812 erupted.

By 1816 Congress passed a law forbidding foreigners to engage in the fur trade, and the British traders congratulated themselves on their prescient move to Kaministiquia. At every fur post in the area strangers were greeted with suspicion as *comis* and voyageurs dreaded the appearance of customs collectors along the ill-defined border area, though no such officials materialized.

Shortly after Hudson's Bay bought out North West in 1821, the American Fur Company entered the area. It had been founded by John Jacob Astor in New York in 1808. Astor was generally credited with lobbying through the legislation prohibiting foreign firms to engage in the fur trade on the as yet unspecified American side. Astor hired successful local traders to work for him, as had North West before him, and used the northwoods fur trade as a springboard to similar operations in Oregon. Astor traded his west-coast furs in China for silk and porcelain, selling these on the American east coast. They were becoming more profitable than furs as fashions changed. Astor's chain of transactions led to one of the greatest New York fortunes of all time. However, his northwoods operations were franchised, and in effect sold, to Hudson's Bay 12 years after they were begun. Slowly but surely the fabulous fur-trade business was becoming marginal.

Astor anticipated trends and fashions; perhaps he helped to create them. Not only were furs getting scarcer owing to the intense trapping and hunting in the northwoods, but as an animal population declined it seemed to become more susceptible to disease, which then hastened the decline. (As twentieth-century ecologists have discovered, the survival of a species depends in part on a sufficiently large genetic pool from which healthy specimen can breed.) Fashions changed from beaver hats and felt to silk. Even the British army stopped using fur hats. The financial panic in 1842 further diminished the demand for fur, and by 1847 Astor's American Fur Company went out of business, having served him well.

The fur trade and the life of the voyageurs continued, though nowhere near the scale of its roaring days when the North West *bourgeois* gathered at Grand Portage. More *hivernauts* were drawn from the *metis* who lived in the area, fewer men came from Montreal. The number of brigades diminished, individual entrepreneurs and fleeting partnerships sought to scrounge a living. It lasted, dwindling and fading, past the American Civil War, and no one knows with certainty when the last *canot du nord* traversed the border lakes, the men chanting *en roulant ma boule* with its endless verses. Perhaps in the 1870s or 1880s. At the beginning of the twentieth century old men in the border country who had paddled in the fur trade still lived there and recalled their life with wistfulness, and lob pines still stood after the old men had died.

But it was not only changing fashions and the diminution of animal population that brought the fur trade to an end. The whole business had depended on Indians who trapped and brought pelts to the posts. The United States established its first Indian Agency at Sault St. Marie in 1822, only a few years after the official exploration parties of Pike and Cass. Treaties were signed with the Ojibway at Prairie du Chien in 1825, at Fond du Lac in 1826, and a more important one in 1837 whereby vast tracts of land were taken by the United States. Especially after 1854 the treaties came with drum-fire speed and the Ojibway were being pushed into ever smaller areas and reservations. Soon fur traders found themselves without regular trappers and put in claims to the United States for credit they had extended to the Indians whom the government had caused to move away before the accounts could be settled.

A hundred years after the great hall of Grand Portage was built the fur trade was dead, the resounding chansons over the lakes a fading memory. A hundred years after the prime of Waubojeeg, one of the greatest Ojibway leaders, the Indians whose trapping, whose development of the portage trails and connecting routes, whose invention of the canoe had made the fur trade possible, had been driven to pauperism and reservations, awaiting a renascence that did not come for almost another hundred years.

Waubojeeg (White Fisher) was born and raised at Chequamaugon. He was over six feet tall, that rarity of natural leader who commands by character and presence. Waubojeeg led the Ojibway in a bloody, decisive battle against the Sioux and Fox at the falls of the St. Croix River, near today's village of Taylors Falls, in 1771 when he was little over 20 years old. The warfare had raged for a long time, and as is so often true in the patterns of history and human relations, the climax came accidentally. War parties, some of them quite large, made annual forays in the struggle for possession of the northwoods. That spring a large party of Sioux and Fox were moving upstream on the St. Croix, headed toward Ojibway villages. Meanwhile a large party of Ojibway led by Waubojeeg were moving downstream and were to be joined by Ojibway from Mille Lacs at St. Croix Falls.

Waubojeeg's scouts saw the enemy first. As the Ojibway landed at the north end of the portage around the falls, Fox and Sioux approached upstream from the south. The two small armies clashed on the cramped trail and among the rocks of the portage. The Sioux sat out the battle in a gesture of bravado and contempt for the Ojibway. As the Fox were being driven into the water, the Sioux changed their minds and joined the melee. Firearms, once emptied, were used as clubs; there was neither time nor space for reloading. The arrival of 15 Ojibway canoes from Mille Lacs helped turn the tide of battle. The carnage was so extreme that the rocks and trails of St. Croix Falls portage were bloodied red; most Sioux and Fox were killed on land or drowned as they were driven into the water. Although no one could have predicted it, the battle was a turning point, a beginning of the end. Ojibway have said since, with more irony than bitterness, that they fought for the country so that the whites could exploit and take it.

With Indian warfare waning, fur trade blossomed. Waubojeeg's leadership among the Lake Superior Ojibway brought stability and a strong sense of spiritual value, for the man who led this bloody battle was poet, singer, and tribal elder. A white trader wanted to marry one of Waubojeeg's daughters. The trader was an unusually well-educated and earnest man, and Waubojeeg told him to return in a year and ask again if he still felt so inclined. Waubojeeg told the man that whites tended to marry Indians for momentary convenience and forsake them. This was commonly the case with voyageurs and traders, but not always. In this instance the trader returned from a winter in Montreal, and Waubojeeg gave his permission.

The couple settled at Sault St. Marie, their children were raised to be bilingual and multicultural, educated in eastern schools and in the Indian traditions when at home. John and Susan Johnston, the trader and Waubojeeg's daughter, were instrumental in saving the members of the Cass Expedition at the Sault in 1820, when a party of Indians wanted to kill them. A few years later their oldest daughter Jane married Henry Schoolcraft, who recorded many of the Ojibway legends and who influenced Longfellow. The chain of human lives reaches beyond the institutions created by man. The imprints of the voyageurs, Indian and French, are on the land and in the historico-moral matrix of the nation.

5

Exploiting the Wilderness

As population, agriculture, and industry expanded in the United States and Canada after the American Civil War, the north-woods between Lake Superior and Lake of the Woods became circumscribed. The rocky terrain of the border-lake country discouraged most settlers and immigrants, who went around the area. A few paid the sporadic *canots du nord* passage money to the Red River or Winnipeg, but most found this too forbidding and long a trip when there were easier ways of reaching the American and Canadian prairies. The north country remained relatively inviolate, the fur trade fallen to low ebb. This changed abruptly in 1870 when the Canadians constructed the Dawson Trail. This patchwork of roads through the border-lake country had been proposed earlier but not much had been done about it.

The Dawson Trail represented an urgent Canadian effort to open the interior and the Northwest to settlement and political control. In 1857 the Hudson's Bay Company charter was destined to lapse and Canadian jurisdiction over the fiefdom seemed feasible. Simon Dawson, surveyor and engineer, and Henry Hind, geologist and naturalist, led one of two parties searching for economical routes west to counter the expansionist aggressions of the Americans as well as any lingering notions the Hudson's Bay governors may have had. Dawson urged a network of brush roads, corduroyed with logs over swampy spots, connecting the bigger lakes where steamboats would ferry travelers. Another expedition proposed a route farther north and less laborious, which was ultimately used for the Transcanadian railroad and highway. Some segments of the Dawson Road were hewed out of the forest, and a tragic rebellion in 1870 brought about the construction of the remainder from Thunder Bay to Winnipeg in three months of heroic effort.

Louis Riel, part Ojibway Indian, Catholic, intellectual mystic at St. Boniface, near Winnipeg, led an armed rebellion of the *metis*, who constituted about half the population of the area and had the support of the mainly Scottish other half. Many of the *metis* were voyageurs who had settled, squatted, in the territory; others were commercial buffalo hunters who supplied the fur trade with pemmican and robes. All, *metis* and Scots, felt threatened by absentee government and the possible loss of their lands. They wanted provincial status and their own elected government. The Canadian government sent a 1,400 man expeditionary force to quell the revolt, and the troops left Thunder Bay on July 1, arriving at Winnipeg August 24, having built the Dawson Road on the way, an incredible achievement considering the terrain. As they hacked their way across country, Riel sent a delegation to make the case for *metis* self-government in Ottawa, where parliament concurred and voted establishment of Manitoba Province and promised amnesty to Riel and his followers. This promise was broken, and Riel had to flee, caught in the crosscurrents of religious and British-French conflicts that are not resolved to this day, and in the conflict between Indian and white, which is also not resolved to this day in Canada as in America. Riel was elected to parliament several times and was never able to take his seat. He studied law, clerked in St. Paul, moved to Montana. Some of Riel's followers fled into the Rainy Lake area and settled, several absorbed by the Indian communities at Red Lake and Nett Lake. In 1884 Canadians and *metis* in Saskatchewan asked Riel to return from Montana and lead their rebellion against the Canadian government. Riel was captured in 1885, tried, and executed as were several of his followers.

The Dawson Road opened to civilian traffic in 1871 for a charge of $25 per person for the 499 miles from Thunder Bay to Winnipeg, half fare for children under 12. Work was begun on a canal at Ft. Frances, 800 feet long and 40 feet wide, with a lock 200 by 38 feet. Work was stopped after most of the excavation was completed in 1878, when a new Canadian government pledged itself to build the more practical Canadian Pacific Railway. The canal can still be seen near the Canadian side of the international bridge at Ft. Frances.

The Dawson Road was so tortuous that after a decade it was no longer used. It entailed 17 changes between steamboats, carts, canoes, stagecoaches, and York boats. Most travelers preferred the longer trip from Montreal to Chicago by a series of steamers, then the train to St. Paul, the stage to Breckenridge, Minnesota, on the Red River, and the sternwheeler to Winnipeg. This was supplanted as the Transcanadian railroad pushed west.

The roundabout route to Winnipeg and Canada's prairies and northwest by way of St. Paul and the Red River Valley had been a problem for Hudson's Bay Company, as well as the Canadian government, and a factor contributing to the demise of the fur trade headquartered in Montreal. A 500-mile trail linking St. Paul and Winnipeg had come into existence in the early 1800s, before either was formally established, over which American goods were hauled to the fur traders, and later the settlers, and furs were brought back on Red River carts—wooden boxes that could be floated across swollen rivers, mounted on two wooden wheels. The first wheels were slices of trees three feet in diameter fastened to unpeeled poplar axles. The screeching noise of the carts was proverbial and usually described as "hellish." Brigades of 10 carts, drawn by horse or oxen, snaked their way along the trail. The value of the traffic grew to $2 million a year, siphoning most of the trade away from Hudson's Bay and Montreal in what was clearly smuggling that no one could stop. Had the Canadians not defeated Riel, whose *metis* outnumbered Canadian whites west of the Great Lakes, American threats to move the boundary up to the 90th

Parallel might well have been made good. As things developed, the Red River trail spurred Canadian development around Winnipeg and in its prairies, hastened the growth of St. Paul into a commercial center, albeit much of its early business was built on smuggling, and speeded the end of Montreal fur trade and the isolation of the border-lakes country.

Even the Ojibway population in the border lakes was on the decline, parallel with the fortunes of the fur trade, and decimated by waves of disease to which there was little immunity. It was American policy to dragnet Indian bands and family groups onto the reservations, continuing the destruction of Indian social and belief systems in a climate of poverty and helplessness. At the same time, the United States was seeking to carve up the reservations into small, individual parcels, many of which could be turned over to white homesteaders and logging firms, and to establish a central location at White Earth to which all Minnesota Indians could be removed. White Earth was situated on the edge of the prairies in western Minnesota, once the buffalo range; near enough to the Red River to be fair farming country, but not in the valley where the soil was good; far enough from the forests and the lakes to compel a different way of life, but still in Minnesota. Most Ojibway resisted the resettlement, and the Indians of Bois Forte and Nett Lake, and Grand Portage, were too far away and isolated to be seriously affected.

In 1865 a gold discovery in the Lake Vermilion area about 100 miles from Rainy Lake brought several hundred prospectors. Some state officials joined in forming a private mining company, and the rush occurred in the dead of winter. Prospectors found no gold, and to this day there is confusion and mystery surrounding the event, speculation that it was a hoax or that interested parties seeded the area and leaked the news to secure financial backing for developing local iron-ore deposits. Gold attracted more excitement and capital than did iron. The Vermilion and later the Mesabi iron ranges began to be mined in the 1880s. Their existence had long been known, but not their extent or richness. Thousands of immigrants now poured into the area within a hundred miles of the border lakes, including Finns, Scandinavians, Slavs, and the ethnic groups from the diverse Austro-Hungarian Empire of the Hapsburgs. The immigrants brought with them a strong desire for freedom and opportunity, political liberalism, and a love of hunting and the outdoors that the aristocratic landowners of the old world would not allow them to put into practice. This passion for the hunt became a continuing tradition, a proprietary concept among their descendants that flared up repeatedly when conservation and park proposals were made. It was matched or exceeded only by the attitudes of the Ojibway, who had been guaranteed perpetual hunting and fishing rights in their treaties with the United States. The area became and still is heavily poached.

Ten years after iron-ore mining began, the annual shipments exceeded 10 million tons a year. Ore was sent overland by rail to newly constructed docks at Two Harbors, a few miles above Duluth on Lake Superior. By then major encroachments were under way on the border lakes and forests.

In 1870 a Scots prospector, Alexander Baker, squatted on the site of today's International Falls. He had to wait more than 10 years before obtaining title, because a survey was required before the deed could be recorded. He was the only resident of Koochiching Falls and sold most of his holding to two Minneapolis speculators soon after he had the deed. The two city men foresaw possibilities in the water power at the falls, which had been described repeatedly in old journals as the most beautiful in the north country, but which are covered now by the backed-up water behind a dam. The speculators recorded their puchase in 1892 and brought in another surveyor to plat a townsite in 1894. Koochiching's plat was filed the same year, but any dreams of carving out a new frontier town were overshadowed by discovery of gold on Rainy Lake islands 11 miles east of Koochiching the previous year.

Over the winter and into the spring of 1894 humanity bypassed Koochiching and poured onto the Kabetogama Peninsula. Covered wagons crossed the prairies from west to east, from the Dakotas to Minnesota; the last several scores of miles over the bog country and through the forest must have been difficult. Others came by foot, on snowshoes, and over the frozen lakes and portages. The nearest railhead was 100 miles southeast at Tower.

Probate Judge John Berg of International Falls recounted his youthful experiences in Rainy Lake City. When he was along in years he prepared his recollections for the Koochiching County Historical Society in 1936, a memoir written with humor and understanding. He had seen the covered Dakota wagons heading eastward, the overnight buildings, log cabins, tents, tar-paper shacks that sheltered more than 500 people in 1894. Entrepreneurs had goods brought laboriously from "outside" except for meat, which the butcher sold: a moose carcass, $5, caribou, $2, and deer, $1. Whitefish, pike, and pickerel sold for 5¢, partridge and duck were for the taking, and there were no game wardens. There were three general stores, a hardware store, a building materials emporium, a butcher shop, a printing office, a bank, three hotels, a barber shop, two restaurants, a post office, a customs office, and five saloons.

The new settlers promptly organized their overnight town, elected a village council, and built a town hall, the back of which served as a jail constructed of "heavy Norway pine logs." The jail had its occasional uses; Rainy Lake City was a friendly community and tended to be nonviolent, but sometimes a friend and neighbor got raucous when inebriated.

Jim Turney, an expert with a Colt .45, had a proclivity for shooting exhibitions after a few drinks. When Patty the Bird walked out of a saloon with a full bottle and proceeded to take a drink from it in the street, Turney shot the bottle out of Patty's hand, breaking the bottle at the neck. Patty fainted. Another townsman was carrying two pails of water up from the lake, when the handle of one was shot off at the fastening without damaging the pail. Looking down at the pail in amazement and then up, he spotted Turney peering from behind a tree 50 feet away. The butcher was also treated to Turney's marksmanship when he did not wait on him fast enough. Turney shot the strings off several rings of sausages hanging from the rafter.

Another town character was Gold Bug Jimmy who lost his way in the woods whenever he strayed from the townsite. Since prospecting was a serious business with Jimmy and he could not pursue it without leaving home, he had to be looked for repeatedly.

Most Rainy Lake City residents who had not come by wagon or canoe arrived from Tower, then the railroad terminus. In winter they traveled over the Lake Vermilion ice to Pelican Lake, by trail to Ash River, then to Kabetogama Lake, across the Nashata Narrows, then to Black Bay and up to townsite. In 1895 the route was shortened by a few miles, but the distance was still close to a hundred miles. In summer small steamboats plied Vermilion, Namakan, Sand Point, and Kabetogama lakes; a stage took travelers and supplies from Vermilion to Crane, then the old Kettle Falls portage was used, and another small steamboat was waiting below on Rainy Lake. The Rainy Lake steamboat was manufactured in Duluth, sailed to Ft. William/Port Arthur, put on railroad cars for Rat Portage (Kenora) on Lake of the Woods, then steamed across the lake and up the Rainy River. At the Koochiching Falls it was hauled up "by main force and awkwardness."

The gold-mining operations were owned by businessmen from Duluth and elsewhere who invested heavily and received little return. It had been expensive to ship mining equipment and machinery over the vexing hundred-mile route from Tower. Once the shafts were sunk and vein rock hauled up and processed, it turned out there was not much gold after all. The Lyle Mine on the north side of Dryweed Island gave out after two years, the Little American after three. Bushy Head mine operated for two years under a superintendent locally known as Bushy Head Johnson. Gold Harbor and Holman functioned for one year.

Little American was the most ambitious. A 200-foot shaft was sunk, then a drift tunnel bored east and west. Ore was taken to the stamp mill near Rainy Lake City by scow. The five-stamp mill worked the ore which had been crushed at mine site, ground it fine, then forced it through a screen onto a copper plate covered with quicksilver which collected the free minerals. The residue was shipped to a smelter for extraction.

The Rainy Lake City bank, like the other businesses, did well during the first flush of high expectations, but fell on lean times as the gold rush dissipated. One day its owner and operator, A. G. Butler of Duluth, rushed out of the bank in the early morning shouting: "Robbers! The bank's been robbed!" The town emptied, armed to the teeth, to scour the woods in all directions. Hours later the posse returned empty-handed and found that Butler had disappeared. He was pursued by canoe and, according to one account, found at the Kettle Falls portage heading toward Tower with the bank's assets. After a spirited debate among members of the posse it was decided to take Butler back to Rainy Lake City where he was made to repay the depositors. "He was set at liberty and disappeared," Judge Berg noted.

A few traces of the mines remain, but Rainy Lake City disappeared almost as fast as it had sprung up, many of its residents and buildings ending up in Koochiching, which was renamed International Falls in 1903.

During its short life the *Rainy Lake Journal* once boasted that at least 2 billion board feet of lumber were accessible in the immediate area. This northwoods boosterism for once understated its case. Small operators had penetrated the border-lakes forests before the start of the century, while the avalanche of large logging companies was rolling northward. The sprinkling of homesteaders grew to fuller volume in 1902-3 as public land sales and homesteading were made easier; pulled by the settlers and pushed by the loggers and the entrepreneurs the railroads came to International Falls in 1907.

Most of the logging took place in winter. Logs were skidded out, often on huge sleds or skids drawn by matched teams of Percherons, immense dray horses each weighing about a ton. At the nearest river or lake the logs were dumped, rafted together in log booms, and floated downstream or pushed by small steamers or alligator boats to the nearest railhead, where hoists pulled and lifted the logs onto railroad cars or to shoresite sawmills. Marking hammers with insignia like cattle brands pounded the logging company's logo into the butt ends of the logs, so they could be sorted by owner. The logos were registered by the state. When the system was working to capacity, one large company was able to ship over 12 million feet of lumber in one season from the Lake Vermilion lakehead. Virginia Rainy Lake Company had 143 logging camps, of which about 40 were within the present park boundaries. Still visible in the park is the railroad grade winding along Ash River into Namakan Lake at Hoist Bay where huge log booms once garnered the big pine. The tracks are long gone, brush has crept up the sides of the embankment, and new forest has recaptured the wasteland of the long-ago logging. At Hoist Bay rotting supports finger out into the lake, which is once more silent save for the sounds of nature.

The logging camps, as had the Iron Range, drew many immigrants, who saw the jobs as a springboard to homesteading. There was much turnover in the workforce. Logging-camp life could be mean and brutal, the work was often dangerous. The pay was not all that good. Some tiny shacks that men lived in were skidded from site to site, dark and overheated and unhealthy. Logging or tote roads were graded as well as they could be so the high skid-loads would not tip over. But a level grade was a rarity in the granite terrain. Hazards ranged from the customary dangers of falling trees and branches to "widow makers," felled trees caught against standing trees, hanging precariously until they crashed down on workmen. Skids did tip, crushing men. Loggers were caught by jammed floating logs and crushed, sometimes drowned. Many of the land-hungry immigrants worked at logging until something better came along. Some divided their time between their struggling homesteads, worked by their families, and the paying jobs they took for a portion of the year. Others were single and footloose, drifting among the camps.

Logging-company managers complained about this unstable work force, but it was not a big problem so long as enough men could be found. Once the trees were gone, the companies would move on. Some of the biggest operators in northern Minnesota made fortunes and then shifted to Oregon and the Northwest. While they were operating in the border-lakes country, some firms advertised widely for immigrants in the United States and Europe. Once the land was cut over the operators moved on. It was up to the help to take its chances and follow the work.

As with other dramatic developments that made a lasting impact, logging of the big timber went on only for several decades. When it was done, the mature pine forests were gone and left were mountains of slashed branches, soil susceptible to erosion, and a dismal fire-prone wasteland awaiting a second growth of aspen, birch, and spruce. Most of it happened in a 30-year-span. A few old men who logged the border country in their youth remember the days of big timber and remaining lob pines. After the last few big log drives in the 1930s, logging was at low ebb until second-growth pulpwood production, scientific forest management, and innovations in the use of wood fibers gradually brought a revival in the 1960s.

When the loggers' caulked boots and their horses' caulked shoes first approached the border lakes to the twang of their six-foot-long two-man saws and the ice-borne resonance of the axes, a brilliant, prescient, and controversial Minneapolis sawmill operator leapfrogged his competitors. Edward W. Backus accurately predicted the future and built a complex of paper mills, power plants, dams, and other enterprises beginning at International Falls. For a time his paper mills were the fourth largest producers in the country.

Backus did much more than beat his competitors in the race for "virgin" timber. He foresaw that riches would come from an enormous increase in the demand for newsprint and paper, and that logging and sawmill operations would be profitable only as secondary enterprises once the land had been cut over. But he also thought that pulpwood was in virtually endless supply from the vast forests on both sides of the border and from regenerating cutover lands. Above all, he valued the role of running water as a power source and an essential element in paper production. He noted the desperation of Canada to develop industry, and recognized that it would be very accommodating to entrepreneurs.

As Backus often told the story, he and his chief timber cruiser snowshoed 200 miles from the end of the railroad line at Brainerd to Koochiching Falls in the winter of 1898, traversing and inventorying timber and water resources as they tramped through the forest land, much of it trackless. When they emerged at the falls, Backus was certain he had found what he had been looking for in the way of plentiful cheap timber, cheap land, and a considerable water flowage for power and paper production.

On his return to Minneapolis, Backus dispatched teams of surveyors and timber cruisers to thoroughly map and inventory the area on both sides of the border. When he had their reports, he sold his interests, made a series of shifting alliances and partnerships, then formed a syndicate. He raised $4 million to construct railroads to the falls site from Brainerd via Bemidji, and from Duluth via Tower. The railroads were completed in 1907. He spent $750,000 of his own money to begin construction of the Koochiching Dam in 1905, complete with a private toll bridge which was still operating in the 1970s as the only crossing between the two countries. The Ontario government was willing to provide extensive pulpwood concessions in return for Backus's promise to build paper mills in Ft. Frances and International Falls. He also obtained rights by lease and by purchase to the potential dam sites along the entire border from Lake Saganaga—which is east of Rainy Lake about 50 miles and now in the Boundary Waters Canoe Area—to Lake of the Woods in the west. At Lake of the Woods he obtained a sawmill and other holdings.

Most foreign investments in Canada in 1900 were British. Soon after the end of World War I over half were American, and Backus had been among the earliest. By 1914 his paper was shipped from International Falls and Ft. Frances mills. By the 1920s he was the fourth-largest paper producer in the United States. He boasted that all north-country wealth and employment came from his vision and gamble, and that when the first train pulled into International Falls at great personal cost and risk, there was nothing to haul except what his vision would provide.

Backus was born in southern Minnesota shortly before the Civil War. His parents were pioneer homesteaders. He attended the University in Minneapolis, working at a variety of jobs, and quit school in his senior year to take over operation of a sawmill where he had been a part-time bookkeeper. He accelerated production, rose to ownership, and by his mid-thirties had become one of the Twin Cities' most substantial businessmen. He saw the Minnesota pineries leveled in the central part of the state and in the Mississippi River Valley, and this triggered his winter explorations through the spruce, pine, aspen, and birch forests in 1898, while his competitors were working their way north.

During his trek that year he crossed the lands of the Leech Lake Indians which had been allotted to individual Indians, but timbering of the prime sawlogs on the "surplus" reservation lands, remaining after the allocations to individuals had been made, was stalemated by disputes over the disposition of the vast acreage. Much of the Indian timber was being pirated, and one of the major logging operators near Leech Lake was Thomas Shevlin, with whom Backus went into partnership when the International Falls enterprises began a few years later. Subsequently Backus went into partnership with William Brooks, businessman, Republican National Committeeman, powerful in Minnesota political circles. Backus also became active in state and national Republican politics, but as it was necessary over the years, he plied both sides of the fence. He promoted Farmer Labor Senator Magnus Johnson for membership on the International Joint Commission regulating boundary waters; Johnson assisted Backus when damage claims were filed after the entrepreneur's dams flooded upstream lands. In neither instance was one successful in aiding the other; Backus would need all the help he could get.

The Backus empire grew and expanded to include real estate, telephone, and railroad companies. He held bank directorships, owned development companies, and sawmills. He was the first to screen paper-mill wastewater and to use the screenings and other byproducts to make insulation. To manage all this, political influence in St. Paul, Washington, and Canada was essential, and Backus cultivated it. At one point President Teddy Roosevelt vetoed, then signed a bill extending time for construction of the Koochiching Dam and thus gave Backus de facto control over the watershed; Minnesota Senator Knute Nelson had intervened on Backus's behalf.

These were times different from the present, with different public mores and values; Backus's attitudes were accepted widely. People smiled tolerantly when he spoke of having "made" the north country, of being entitled to take advantage of cheap land, cheap timber, and cheap labor, of taking the water and the subsidy of two nations to his personal gain. This was an age far removed from today's efforts to balance environmental values with economic profit.

Power dams were vital to Backus, as he saw it. He had hidden the Koochiching Falls behind a dam, raising the Rainy Lake level several feet. Other dams were built at Lake of the Woods, and at Kettle Falls, which also raised water levels and flooded lands. He had plans to build more. At Little Vermilion, Curtain Falls, Basswood, Saganaga, Kawnipi, Maligne, Lac la Croix, at Winton and at Gabbro Lake. Had all of these been built, much of what is now

Boundary Waters Canoe Area within the Superior National Forest would have been under water. Lower Basswood Falls, for instance, would have been drowned out; Silver Falls at Saganaga would have disappeared. Ironically, Backus was absolutely convinced that his success and his future depended on these dams, and they probably were not necessary at all.

The dams, and even more Backus's arrogance, led to mounting difficulties and court cases, some over trivialities, many unnecessary. A widow who rented a parcel of land to Backus was mulcted and sued him; upriver landowners who had been flooded out had to sue for damages; a year after the partnership terminated, Backus blocked a Shevlin log drive on the Big Fork, and when the Shevlin foreman broke through the illegal barrier across the river, Backus had him arrested for trespass. Perhaps it was thought ridiculous that such a powerful man would stoop to capricious and malicious petty mischief. In time, when major court cases and international issues came before tribunals and the future of Backus's entire empire was at stake, he had a reputation that hurt him and alienated the carefully cultivated political support when he needed it most.

The disputes about dam construction, flooding, and water levels, instead of being assuaged by the payment of claims and a spirit of compromise, erupted into the courts and finally came to the six-member International Joint Commission in two formal References in 1912 and 1925. For a Reference to come before the commission, both countries had to agree that it should be heard. The 1912 Reference stemmed from a deadlock between competing, conflicting interests over control of the border-lakes waters. Duluth wanted to divert water for its own power purposes—it was even contemplating a canal to do so, if necessary. This would have taken water that Backus and other logging interests wanted and depended on. However, the timbermen and, to the west, Winnipeg interests opposed Backus's plans, which interfered with their own. The International Joint Commission heard the arguments and issued a ruling in 1917, at the height of World War I production.

The IJC opinion left the Duluth proposal high and dry, and addressed itself to stabilizing Lake of the Woods water levels. The outlets there could be enlarged, power capacity increased, and the door was open for Backus to extend power development beyond Koochiching and Kettle Falls far into the watershed, though the report failed to specify who would pay for all of this, or who would be responsible, and to what extent, for damages to owners of flooded property. This was half a loaf for Backus, who had also hoped to be relieved of the cost of the dams and of the mounting damage claims.

Backus roared into the opening created by the Lake of the Woods Reference. He purchased the Lake of the Woods dams at the outlets, agreed to build a pulp mill, and got the rights to the timber around the lake. But when he sought dam sites on the upstream lakes from the Canadians at Little Vermilion, Loon, LaCroix, Crooked, Knife, and Saganaga, he failed. His request to raise water levels 30 feet on Saganagons, Kawnipi, and Sturgeon was not answered. He did obtain some other sites and bullied the Ontario government into a major timber concession by personally joining 500 people demonstrating on behalf of this lease in Toronto. It was suggested he had organized the demonstration and had helped pay for it. It obtained the results he desired.

He sought absolute control over the watershed through an international treaty, but failed, despite vigorous pulling at political strings. In court he fought to protect himself against damage assessments, and lost. He felt he needed protection against such assessments if he were to build any more dams, as well as cost sharing from the governments, because his activities constituted a public beneficence. The second Reference thus came to the International Joint Commission in 1925, and was called the Rainy Lake Reference to distinguish it from the earlier one. It was to deal with the flowage rights and protection from damages.

Backus was 65 when the hearings began. Perhaps with age his irascibility, pride, and self-righteousness were heightened, for he demanded and expected that two governments would underwrite and guarantee his further expansions, that an international tribunal would safeguard him against damages, and that he would not have to submit hard cost figures for all of this, his word and that of his influential friends and minions being sufficient. For the first time, the larger public began to see Backus not as a colorful individualist who did much good in his own sharp way, but as a man indulging personal greed at public expense and causing damage for which he did not want to make restitution.

At the Rainy Lake Reference hearings Backus had opposition. The city of Ft. Frances objected because city sewers would be flooded by higher Rainy Lake water levels. Winnipeg companies said they did not need more power, and if Backus wanted money to build more dams that would benefit only him, he should pay for them. Backus disdained this line of argument and did not submit firm cost figures. For the first time, conservationists fought Backus for despoiling the countryside and doing damage to the public assets and future prospects by ruining the beauty and ecological balance of a unique area.

It was a calculated risk for anyone to oppose Backus, and it was done with a great deal of fear and trepidation, justifiably as it turned out. Lawyers in the ranks of the conservationists were called by clients who urged them not to interfere. Bankers, insurance people, and others got the message indirectly that it just was not wise to thwart Backus. Some who heard this message but did not heed it had their bank notes called in. A man so powerful as to have an audience in the highest circles of industry and two governments, a man with a long record of vindictiveness in even petty matters, was not opposed with impunity.

Izaak Walton spokesman Howard Selover testified that Backus's proposed dams would destroy the remaining beauty of the land. The Arrowhead Association said there was "no money that can repay the American people for the destruction." The Lake County Commissioners said there was nothing in Backus's proposals that would benefit *their* industry or taxes.

Central to the opposition was the testimony of Ernest C. Oberholtzer. He and Backus lived on neighboring islands on Rainy Lake, within sight of each other, sometimes socialized in the small community, yet were at opposite poles over what constituted the public interest and the best future of the north.

"When you destroy the beauty of that region, you destroy its utility," Oberholtzer declared. His carefully prepared testimony at the hearings was devastating to Backus's case.

The organization of conservationists, and their opposition to

Backus, began a conflict that did not abate until Backus died nine years after the second Reference was heard. It was a very bitter life-and-death struggle, yet some civilities were observed. Backus made a formal annual call on his neighbor Oberholtzer, without fail. Imperious, a powerful presence compared to the small Oberholtzer, Backus would arrive impeccably dressed to pay his respects, and leave.

The Rainy Lake Reference final report was not issued until July 1934. It emerged during the Depression. Newell Searle, in his book *Saving Quetico-Superior: A Land Set Apart*, says that "somewhere between 1925 and 1934 lay a watershed in public thinking, and the report reflected the shifting values."

The commission's findings went against Backus, maintaining the status quo. This disappointed the conservationists as well, but the practical effect was that it prevented further dambuilding.

Backus had borrowed too much, as had other industrialists, and he had overexpanded. Finally the setbacks in the courts, before the commission, and elsewhere took their cumulative toll as did the national economic downturn. Backus's political support had eroded for the same reasons, and he could no longer call on the state Republican apparatus, or Washington, for help—actually they could not have assisted him when the banks began calling in notes and there was insufficient cash to pay them. His holdings went into receivership. He fought desperately, frantically to regain control. In 1934 he was 74, charging that eastern bankers had conspired to grasp his hard-earned conglomerate, that the receivers were cheating him and ruining what he had spent a lifetime developing. He obtained a hearing before the U.S. Senate banking and currency committee, failing to establish his claims, kept struggling, and died of a heart attack in a New York hotel room in the fall of 1934 on yet another sortie to recoup.

Backus's enterprises, the Minnesota and Ontario paper and power complex, survived the Depression under new owners and went on to prosper without the added dams. In 1965 M & O was acquired by Boise Cascade. For decades the industries that Backus founded were the major economic force in the area. Far to the southeast, the Iron Range was exploited to exhaustion during two world wars until it seemed that the mining industry was destined to atrophy and die. The introduction of taconite mining, extracting lower-grade ore, revitalized it. Elsewhere in the larger region there was nickel mining, near Atikokan, Ontario. Winnipeg had grown into a major commercial and educational center, feeding and being fed by the prairies. Duluth was revitalized by construction of the St. Lawrence Seaway and became a major port for grain from the Midwest, iron ore, and other goods. The cities of Ft. William and Port Arthur, the Kaministiquia of fur-trade days, joined under the name Thunder Bay and became a thriving city. But it required many years for these things to happen.

During the decades of the Depression and the years that followed, much of the north country had an aura of orphaned boomtowns. This was the result of the brief springtime honeymoon of big timber, which disappeared so quickly; of farms established after backbreaking toil succumbing to thin soil and short growing seasons; of resorts and tourism built on little capital done in by depreciation, poor fishing, altering tastes and technologies such as camping vehicles and canoeing.

The hardy people had tried many things. Maple-syrup manufacture, commercial fishing, caviar production based on a diminishing number of lake sturgeon, small manufacturies, summer camps, stores, and businesses. They tried consumer cooperatives and producer cooperatives, federal assistance and self-help.

During the 1930s Civilian Conservation Corps camps dotted the north country. Unemployed men from Kansas, New York, Chicago, and elsewhere came to fight forest fires that were fed by the accumulation of slash left by the loggers. CCCs planted new forests which seemed a drop in the bucket after the timbering. But in a few years the countryside changed for the better and regreened with pine. The burden of tax-forfeited lands was converted into state forests and parks. Large firms in the paper and wood products field purchased tracts and planted trees. The twin arrows of the Tree Farm signs became commonplace. The homogeneous forests of red pine opened the prospect of disease that a heterogeneous forest could throw off, but that was in the far future. The absolute control of forest fires deprived the land of the natural and beneficial effects fire has always had in a completely wild and natural environment.

It was a peculiar economy that emerged in the northland, teetering on the brink of solvency, supersensitive to every fluctuation in the national business cycles, so sparsely populated as to get last and least consideration. Changes occurred subtly and indiscernibly at first. Children born from the 1950s on never saw the wasteland of the 1930s; they grew up in a world of green forests. Affluence elsewhere and changing tastes and values brought city people to newly purchased lakeshore lots, once again threatening the beauty and ecological integrity of the land; some city people were dismayed with urban life and moved north, hoping to find jobs. The Indian reservations, quiescent and poverty stricken for so long, somehow beat the rest of the country to the trough of antipoverty programs and other federal assistance. Activity and money flowed from Grand Portage, Nett Lake, and Red Lake to build houses and start businesses, and the Indians hired whites. With the Indian renascence came power and acumen, and they successfully sued for exclusive hunting and fishing rights guaranteed them on their lands by treaties. College-trained Indian professionals came home to the reservations to teach, work, and lead, instead of seeking middle-class anonymity in the cities. Indians successfully competed for jobs outside the reservations. The vigor and aggressiveness of the Indians, and their successes, startled the surrounding communities. There was an implied, indirect message from the Indians to the larger community: a decent, wholesome life required both respect for the land and nature, and economic vitality; either without the other was insufficient and sometimes destructive; both depended on respect for the life processes in oneself, in others, in nature, wherever they existed.

Could it be that both Backus and Oberholtzer had been right, had somehow been on the edge of a great truth?

6

Birth of a Park

In the early afternoon session of the Minnesota Legislature on Wednesday, April 1, 1891, Representative G. J. Lomen from St. Paul's 1st Ward rose to introduce a resolution calling for establishment of a national park on the northern border with Canada. Lomen's proposal pointed to the existence of more than 3 million acres of land not yet settled along the Rainy River and Rainy Lake, and indicated that there should be such a park stretching from Lake Vermilion to Lake of the Woods, a distance of over 100 miles, because this was the kind of land that Congress had intended for parks when it delegated to the president the right of setting apart lands not yet settled that "will contribute to the general welfare."

These lands, Lomen's draft resolution informed the House, were mainly "non-arable" and could be "better forested to *promote rainfall* and humidity in our atmosphere, to the advantage of agri-

culture . . . and add to the beauty of the state and the healthful-
ness of the climate."

Resolutions often have hidden agenda and implied content; Lomen's was no exception. Underlying the reference to promoting
rainfall was an entire theory of forestry and agriculture that had
gained vogue since 1864. One of its basic concepts was that shelter-
belts of forest helped to ensure moisture and good air for nearby
agricultural areas. Southern Minnesota was farmbelt, Minneapolis
and St. Paul were the grain-milling centers with interests reaching
far into the prairies, and both groups were favorably inclined to
having forests that ensured rain. The farmlands were being deep-
plowed, disrupting moisture cycles and water tables, and were
proving vulnerable to drought and dust storms. There had been
subsidies for planting trees, arbor days, and farmers were urged to
plant trees at least in and about the farmyards. A few complaints
that public expenditure for reforestation, tree planting, and parks
was "socialism" did not generate support; general sentiment was
in favor of keeping Minnesota green.

Forestry, forest management, and the creation of parks were
new interests in the 1890s, in Minnesota, the country, and the
world. One of the pioneers in the field of forestry was Christopher
C. Andrews of Minnesota, and the views and interests of Andrews
and his friends were well and clearly expressed in the Lomen Resolution, which said that the proposed national park should have
"provisions for protection against depredation and fires, and for
reforestation of denuded sections, as will constitute it one of the
great forest retreats of the country."

The resolution provided that the governor, the secretary of the
State Board of Agriculture, and the secretary of the State Forestry
Association (of which Andrews was a founder) would constitute a
committee for a Minnesota national park, to obtain a survey and
to lobby for its establishment.

Lomen had been elected as a Republican, swamping his Prohi-
bitionist Party opponent. At the time, the northern counties were
so sparsely settled that Beltrami County ran from Lake Itasca to
Lake of the Woods, and the official state map shows only two
lumber camps and Ponemah Village on Red Lake Reservation.
Itasca County began at Mille Lacs and went north to the border at

Rainy Lake and Rainy River. The advancing avalanche of logging was sweeping northward in 1891, had passed Brainerd, and was approaching Bemidji. But it was still 100 miles short of the Canadian border. Not many people were familiar with the border country even then.

The legislature's reception of Lomen's resolution was friendly, but he was asked to amend it and bring it back the next day. He did, changing the minimum size of the requested park from "not less than ten thousand acres" to forty thousand. Ten thousand would have been a drop in a bucket of 3 million, and even forty thousand was small. The House passed the resolution, and on April 18 the Senate concurred. In short order the governor approved and the secretary of state, F. P. Brown, formally forwarded Minnesota's request for a national park on its border with Canada to the Congress, the Department of the Interior, and the president, none of whom acted on it. Concurrently the state legislature dealt with related concerns. On April 20, 1891, it gave final approval to the law establishing Itasca State Park encompassing the Mississippi River headwaters and source lakes. Itasca's creation had the assistance of some of the executives of the logging company that had cut over most of the area, and who later donated 3,000 acres to enlarge the park. The donation included groves of mature red and white pine which were impressive then and which today constitute a living cathedral as they tower on the lakeshore.

Other state parks followed Itasca, even though the proposal for a national park on the border lakes was ignored in Washington. A healthy state forestry movement came into being, one of the earliest in the nation. C. C. Andrews's campaign on behalf of forest management, including timber management, recreation values, and conservation persuaded others to join him. Then a tragedy galvanized public and political support for the forestry movement. A fire at Hinckley, Minnesota, in 1894, fueled in part by the residual slash of bygone logging, caused over 400 deaths. Long, and sometimes acrimoniously debated issues were legislated quickly in the wake of the fire, including a still functioning state fire-warden system. Public debate and the gradual and cumulative formation of public opinion led the state to a firm commitment to resources management and conservation, and this process as well as its results were to be formative 60 and 70 years later when Voyageurs National Park was being considered, promoted, and finally approved. The Minnesota National Forest, later known as the Chippewa National Forest, began as a Minnesota proposal for another national park.

The Dawes Act of 1887 allotted reservation lands to individual Indians and made it possible for the government to sell or offer for homesteading the balance of what had before been communally owned by the Indians. The stated intent was to "civilize" Indians by abolishing their sovereignty. While all Minnesota Indians had seen their land base shrink in treaty after treaty, and then shrink further as a result of the Dawes Act, Leech Lake Reservation in the north-central part of the state, and about 100 miles south of the border lakes, became the center of a storm. It was a huge reservation and after allotment, large tracts of land remained as "surplus." Leech Lake Ojibway stemmed from several bands, some of whom had been removed to White Earth Reservation a few years before in an abortive attempt to dragnet all Minnesota Indians and encapsulate them there—but they returned home. The divided Indians were voiceless pawns in the developments that all but destroyed their home base at Leech Lake.

A stalemate developed over how to dispose of the "surplus" lands, during which time much of its prime timber was plundered. A brief armed rebellion led by Bugonageshik, in which a U.S. Army detachment was defeated and suffered several casualties in 1898, highlighted the frustration and drew more public attention; the timber irregularities became a public scandal. When the General Land Office announced it would sell 100,000 acres in May 1899, concerned citizens formed an organized lobby for a national park. C. C. Andrews, now the state fire warden, recommended that all the Leech Lake lands be made a state park. He decried the practice of setting fires so that loggers could cut "dead and down" timber to sell to the large lumber companies run by Thomas H. Shevlin and Thomas B. Walker, and others. The powerful Federation of Women's Clubs had called for investigations of these logging abuses and now demanded a national park, a cause joined by federations in other states. Vigorous lobbying brought suspension of the land sale and the battle of the Minnesota National Forest was on. At the time, the distinction between forest and park had not yet been made; this was the *cause célèbre* that brought it about.

The tug of war between local residents, lumber companies, downstate conservationists, out-of-state park champions, state, and federal officials, made for fluctuating battle lines. Feelings ran deep because they touched everyone's economic needs and expectations, and touched class and social differences. The war was waged in newspapers, in leaflets, flyers, and cartoons. There was extensive lobbying. In the end a compromise was fashioned by Gifford Pinchot and others. Pinchot headed the Forestry Bureau of the U.S. Agriculture Department, then a small information agency that obtained its first legislated field mission with the Minnesota Forest to become the U.S. Forest Service in 1905 (the National Park Service was formed as such in 1916).

Pinchot drew on the experience of Herman H. Chapman, then head of the University of Minnesota experimental forestry station at Grand Rapids. Chapman knew that the land would not lend itself to clearing and farming, information which the businessmen boosters of Cass Lake and Bemidji would not yet accept. Chapman also realized that the big-timber operators would oppose a 4-million-acre national park as a "Chinese wall," but that at least some of them would support a national forest that would permit logging and that pursued scientific forest management. Chapman painstakingly developed a forest reserve plan, Duluth Congressman Page Morris, who earlier had opposed conservation measures, introduced it, and Pinchot called interested parties to meetings to work out the compromise, aided by the vigorous Florence E. Bramhall of the Women's Federation. The Morris Bill passed in 1902. It opened large parcels to logging and then farming, and put 225,000 acres in the forest reserve. This national forest had within it a set-aside for experimental forestry, minimum standards for logging elsewhere, and included for recreation some Cass Lake and Leech Lake areas of great beauty. Everyone was happy, except the disfranchised Indians, and no one realized the patterns and precedents that had been set. Over the decades the size of the Chippewa National Forest, so named officially in 1928, doubled, and the erosion of remaining Indian lands was stopped or slowed under the New Deal.

The creation of the first legislated national forest set a profound precedent for public land use and management, although at the time no one could possibly have realized this. It was seen as a political compromise. The function of the Forest Service as conservationists on a large scale had as yet to evolve and develop, but the foundation was there.

The Chippewa National Forest had scarcely been established in 1902, when the man who had much to do with the 1891 national parks resolution behind the scenes, and who was also involved in the movement to save the Leech Lake forests, conceived of yet another crusade. He set the wheels in motion for what would become the Superior National Forest, with its one of a kind enclave—the Boundary Waters Canoe Area and the Quetico-Superior.

C. C. Andrews was 76 in 1905, but age did not stop this patron saint of north-country conservation from going on a canoe trip from Basswood to Crane Lake or from beginning yet another campaign. He so admired the beauty of the wooded, rocky lake and river country and the forested islands and lakeshores that on his return he recommended that the federal government set aside major portions because "to denude them of timber would be of public injury." The General Land Office withdrew over 100,000 acres from sale and eventually Andrews and his supporters prevailed in having President Theodore Roosevelt establish the Superior National Forest in 1909. From a small beginning, the Superior has gradually grown until it now reaches from Grand Portage Reservation on Lake Superior to the boundaries of today's Voyageurs Park, but it did not happen easily and overnight. And within the Superior Forest is the Boundary Waters Canoe Area, safeguarded as wilderness by law.

The Superior Forest now encompasses over 1 million acres along about 160 miles of border from Grand Portage to Crane Lake. The benchmark developments in this sporadic, sometimes faltering growth from Andrews's first recommendation in 1902 were Land Office set-asides that year and in 1905, and establishment of the National Forest in 1909 (with the Canadians matching it on their side with park status for the Quetico). In 1926 Interior Secretary Jardine designated it a roadless area, one of the first clear victories for Oberholtzer and his friends. Then came the

Shipstead-Nolan Act of 1930, providing legislative mandate for managing the National Forest as a wilderness recreation area. Rulings by the International Boundary Commission in effect stopped any further tampering with boundary-water levels and dam construction, but refused to overturn any earlier changes (making Backus and the conservationists unhappy). In 1934 a presidential Quetico-Superior Committee was established, spurring federal land purchases for the checkerboarded forest. The Thye-Blatnick Act of 1948 further bolstered wilderness and roadless status, and in 1949 President Truman banned airplane flights into the area by executive order. The Multiple Use Act of 1960 broadened federal wilderness and recreation policies to all federal lands, and this was capped by the Wilderness Act of 1964 which made it national policy; ironically the Superior National Forest was exempted from some of its provisions because that precedent-setter had accumulated so many compromises on the way that they could not be obliterated by the new law. However, the Superior National Forest, bellwether and lightning rod of conservationists across the country for half a century, had made conservation a matter of national conscience, a matter of setting national priorities and making commitments. This happened because each decision in the long chain involved choosing either the values of wilderness, nature, and aesthetics or the value of more immediate profit. Minnesota's wilderness, which had prompted the distinction of national park from national forest, had brought about another major option: valuing wilderness and recreation in its forests and as a national goal. Across the line on the map where the Superior National Forest ended and Voyageurs National Park would one day begin such decisions had yet to be made.

The collision of Backus and the conservationists was avoided for a while as he concentrated on the western half of the border lakes area, and they on the eastern. The inevitable conflict came over the middle ground, then broadened to the integrity and quality of the environment of a larger area, and lasted for decades.

As noted earlier, Backus symbolized industrial development of the border-lakes country and Ernest Oberholtzer became a symbol and spokesman for the naturelovers—and after Oberholtzer, geologist and author Sigurd Olson. Oberholtzer was a generation younger than Backus and came from Davenport, Iowa. He studied landscape architecture at Harvard and gravitated to the north country on canoe trips, taking photographs and studying Ojibway history and culture, all of which became lifelong pursuits. Short and slightly built compared to the stocky Backus, and with different lifestyle, values, and associations, Oberholtzer did have some qualities in common with his older symbolic counterpart. Each was certain of his righteousness, disinclined to compromise, and reluctant to suffer opponents and differences of view gladly. Neither was known to be very diplomatic, although both were politically effective at times.

In countryside never far removed from the pioneer ethos, Backus and Oberholtzer played out their long lifetimes as legendary characters while confrontations ranged the forums from local and state bodies to involve Congress, the Joint International Commission, presidents, premiers, Minnesota political parties, and assiduously wooed public opinion. Backus died in 1934, Oberholtzer in 1977, and although each may have felt he did not achieve what he had set out to do, the empire founded by Backus is thriving and the integrity of the wilderness of the Superior and its Boundary Waters Canoe Area, and now of Voyageurs, is intact or within reach of being made whole.

From the 1920s to passage of the Wilderness Act in 1964 many famous people were drawn into the fight on behalf of conservation. C. C. Andrews died in 1922, having achieved a great deal for resource preservation, forestry, and the safeguarding of wilderness. Arthur Carhart, a young landscape architect, gave early and prophetic shape to the recreational aspects of the Superior and then to the Forest Service as a whole. Aldo Leopold became an early and long-time supporter. But during the nearly 50 years of contest over the Quetico-Superior it was Oberholtzer who testified at hearings, conducted the correspondence and organizational work and some of the moneyraising, closely helped by a tightly knit, small circle of friends in Minneapolis and Chicago.

Backus began to lose ground before the International Boundary Commission and in the courts, but his home base at International Falls continued to grow, as did the subsidiaries. Paper-mill and wood-processing facilities expanded, and the town that often records the lowest winter temperatures in the continental United States became a hub for tourism and resort activities. Cabins and summer homes sprang up on Rainy and Kabetogama Lakes and some of the islands. Most were modest but a few were sumptuous and usable year round. Gravel pits and garbage dumps developed not too far from the Kabetogama south shore, and canoeists venturing past the Boundary Waters into Rainy and Kabetogama mingled with motorboats. When the wind was right, the sulphur fumes and dust from International Falls and Ft. Frances plants wafted the 20 miles to Kabetogama and beyond, and in the other direction the waters of Rainy River became seriously polluted.

Oberholtzer, his friends, companions, and confederates, nourished an ambitious dream. They wanted to see tremendous international preservation of the entire border-lakes area as a wilderness —on both sides of the border—anchored by a treaty between the United States and Canada. The American Legion endorsed and supported this proposal as a memorial to those Americans and Canadians who served in World War I, and later, in the second World War. Conservationists and some businessmen also backed the idea. Like the champions of the Minnesota National Forest at Leech Lake 25 years before and 100 miles south, they were adamant in their desire to preserve and protect the natural beauty and processes. Yet even the dreamers had to acknowledge the reality of industrial development as a human necessity: so many thousands of square miles could not be walled off into a parklike wilderness. As with the Leech Lake precedent, Oberholtzer and his friends were compelled to compromise time and again, to build on the piecemeal foundation of the Superior National Forest, then the Boundary Waters Canoe Area enclave within it, and eventually Voyageurs National Park. The westernmost park boundary was still 100 miles short of their initial dream, and on the Canadian side even less was accomplished except for the establishment of Quetico Park by the Province of Ontario. Their hopes for a binational treaty and Canadian counterparting did not materialize beyond this, and Canadian industrial and lakeshore development became a major threat not only to their dream, but also to the environmental quality of the region. However, their building-block pioneering did help pace the area and the nation to the wilderness and environmental protection laws, and to the national policies of the 1960s and 1970s.

Both Oberholtzer and his friends, and Backus, had begun with gigantic canvases on which to emblazon their vision of the world. Both had to retrench. Backus had been driven back from his ambitious dams and power network, out of the Superior Forest. Although he died exhausted by the years of court cases, commission hearings, and his own intransigence, his successors continued to build the complex Minnesota and Ontario firm, which later became part of Boise Cascade. It diversified, modernized, and sought to come to grips with the increasing requirements for protection of the environment. Oberholtzer and the conservationists evolved their views of what constituted a responsible public management of the border lakes and forests; they shifted from a stand for completely roadless wilderness to one that incorporated logging areas, some roads, and some industry, so long as the lakeshores and watersheds were completely protected. Backus's canvas shrank to the heartland of his enterprises, from Kettle Falls to Lake of the Woods; Oberholtzer's concerns became primarily those from Grand Portage to about Kettle Falls, if rough and arbitrary lines have to be drawn. Oberholtzer grumbled about the compromises and the half measures, unassuaged by the precedents he and his associates had helped to set. The champions of the Quetico-Superior were exhausted and broke, the notion of an International Peace Memorial Forest no longer taken seriously. However, repeated battles and issues about the quality of the environment in the Superior Forest would rally the faithful: Just where should logging be permitted? Where should the Boundary Waters Canoe Area boundaries be set? Should any mining be allowed? The brushfires erupt to the present day.

Minnesota never gave up its efforts to secure a national park, even though the 1891 resolution had been greeted by silence, and the original park proposition for the Minnesota National Park had somehow devolved into that new institution, a national forest. With the dogged persistence that every nationality considers uniquely its characteristic, Minnesotans suggested a national park at Ft. Snelling, the confluence of the Minnesota and Mississippi

Rivers near the Twin Cities; but during its early years the Park Service had yet to discover the advantages of small parks, historic sites, monuments, and recreation areas near population centers. Itasca was proposed several times and turned down because it was considered inadequate, although the final verdict is not in since there are major parcels of state parklands and other tracts adjacent to the Mississippi headwaters park. Park Service studies in the 1930s showed that the Kabetogama-Rainy Lake area might make a very suitable national park, particularly if linked with the Superior National Forest and perhaps Grand Portage Reservation: this did not arouse much enthusiasm among the Grand Portage Indians, and the Forest Service was not inclined to surrender its cornerstone or to enter into any cooperative agreements controlling its operations.

In 1948 the Minnesota and Ontario Paper Company suggested an exchange of its very substantial land holdings on Kabetogama Peninsula, much of it cut over, for considerably smaller acreage of state-owned spruce forest. The state was interested and held hearings, aware that such a land exchange could provide the basis for a state park to be turned over eventually to a national park. However a number of conservation-oriented witnesses expressed their suspicions of the offer, which was subsequently withdrawn.

Throughout the '50s the name of Kabetogama reappeared among Minnesota suggestions, as did Itasca, the Northwest Angle on Lake of the Woods, and the North Shore of Lake Superior. The Northwest Angle was turned down because of size, remoteness, and the adamant refusal of the Red Lake Indians (who own portions of it) to even consider such an arrangement. The Lake Superior shore offered many stretches of spectacular scenery and was still relatively pristine in the '50s, though the presence of taconite-processing plants and transportation facilities was imminent and would intrude on this landscape. By the '60s there was still no Park Service action on a national park in Minnesota, though the Kabetogama area was again found to have good potential. A 1960 Park Service update survey of its extensive 1938 study of Minnesota park, parkway, and recreation potentials cited Kabetogama as "perhaps possessing national park potential."

The Minnesota park movement was separate from the efforts of

Oberholtzer and the Quetico-Superior movement, which focused specifically on the border lakes and, ultimately, on the Superior Forest and BWCA, to which it drew a national following. Although not mutually exclusive, some membership overlapped, the Minnesota Parks Division (later a part of the Department of Natural Resources) and the private Minnesota Council of State Parks pursued establishment of various state parks and kept the notion of a national park alive.

The people who were drawn to these efforts were mainly successful professional men in the cities. Judge C. R. Magney, for instance, led a one-man campaign to have the Park Service declare Grand Portage a National Monument, a step that facilitated reconstruction of the Great Hall and maintenance of the nine-mile trail from Lake Superior to the Pigeon River, where Ft. Charlotte had once stood. Judge Magney was motivated by a love for the beauty of the north country, and a conviction that without parks and their statutory function of preserving wilderness, historic sites, and places of unusual value, this beauty would be dissipated and destroyed under private ownership and exploitation.

"The Minnesota scenery on the basis of quality and diversity compares favorably with the rest of the world," Judge Magney said, and repeated to whoever would listen.

Erick Kendall was born in Finland and came to the United States in his late teens in 1923. A journalist and editor active in the Wisconsin and Minnesota cooperative movement, Kendall had traveled throughout the world. He supported the park movement because "I had never before, nor since, seen lakes and forested shores as breathtakingly magnificent as the border lakes, although I came from a land of lakes, rivers, and waterfalls." When the time came again for the Voyageurs Park to be seriously considered, Kendall campaigned for it untiringly and ultimately won the support of the Midland Cooperative, consisting of 350,000 members.

Hennepin County Municipal Judge Edwin P. Chapman was a persistent speaker and proponent of expanding state parks, and of securing a national park in the Kabetogama area. Chapman, Magney, and others felt that the Kabetogama park was too big for the state to handle, and that the National Park Service would be able to do a better job of it.

During the 1930s, the National Park Service conducted a cooperative project with various states to develop state park and recreation plans. These were to be long-range plans that could be used by states as a basis for their own park development, and could also serve to identify possible future national-park sites. The supervisor of the Minnesota project was U. W. Hella, who transferred from the Park Service to the Minnesota Parks Division in 1938, which he eventually came to head. On one trip to the Kabetogama area, Hella checked on the lands around Black Bay because highway construction was being proposed that would bridge the neck of the bay and extend a road onto the peninsula itself.

"Fortunately the bridge construction never materialized," Hella recalls of this 1939 visit, "and my report did recommend acquisition of shoreline lands in order to preserve the natural scene."

Hella became head of the Minnesota Parks Division in 1953, after a 12-year absence from the organization. Under his direction, the state park system expanded; small parks were developed along the North Shore of Lake Superior, safeguarding portions of the spectacular scenery, but a national park still proved elusive, however Hella and others tried. He was firmly convinced that Kabetogama was an ideal site, as was the Northwest Angle on Lake of the Woods, where Verendrye and his men had established one of their posts. Undaunted by the reluctance of the federal government to go ahead, Hella kept building the state park system and renewed his proposals to Washington from time to time.

Hella, Magney, and Chapman had support and encouragement from out-state associates such as Harold Bishop, a Park Rapids merchant, Dr. Norman Baker, a Fergus Falls physician, and out-of-state vacationers.

Feeling that the 1939 Minnesota State Park Plan had become outdated, Hella contacted the National Park Service in 1957 for assistance in devising a new plan, and National Park staff were dispatched to tour the state with him during two successive summers. Hella took the opportunity to once again suggest that they keep their eyes open for possible national-park sites.

The 1960 gubernatorial election in Minnesota was close, but Elmer L. Andersen, a veteran state senator, successful businessman, civic leader and longtime participant in several social and humanitarian projects, took office in 1961. Minnesota political tradition in mid-century hewed to a parameter of competent, moderate men, and the string of governors drawn from both parties tended to value economic development in balance with environmental protection, expansion and improvement of educational and social services, and sound management (however much each political candidate found his opponent lacking). When Andersen took office, northern Minnesota was in serious economic straits. What farming economy there had been was shattered beyond remedy, and hundreds of families had vacated the marginal land. The resort and tourism industry was, for many resort operators, marginal; the beginnings of the camping vogue and vacation vehicles, such as campers, were being felt. The logging industry, mainstay of the north, was experiencing the national economic pinch, and the paper companies that purchased large amounts of pulpwood were face to face with the consequences of several years during which they had not expanded or modernized facilities—this would now be much more expensive because of the new emphasis on environmental protection, at a time when capital investment had been postponed too long. There was not much Andersen could do about the multi-national, long-term problems of the paper industry, or about the lassitude of the national economy. But it seemed reasonable to assume that the problems of northeastern Minnesota would lend themselves to amelioration by the state.

Andersen devised a two-pronged effort that was carefully thought out, the tactics orchestrated in detail: encouragement of the taconite industry as a source of employment, and establishment of a system of national and state parks as an inducement to tourism. Both campaigns were laid out to be nonpartisan, to draw on the perceived advantages to the largest number of people and interest groups, and to avoid past political pitfalls. As Andersen saw it, neither effort could succeed without the other, for to turn all northern Minnesota into parkland was not feasible; and to promote a major industry in spectacular countryside without an environmental and aesthetic offset was unthinkable. Besides, both tourism and jobs were needed for a balanced economy. The same process of weighing and juxtaposing factors that had gone into the creation of the Minnesota National Forest was being brought into play, though the participants may not have been aware that they were drawing on a tradition that had been formulated in their state 60 years before. Andersen and his associates tended to view themselves as pragmatists with a social conscience, concerned with practicalities and the here and now.

The taconite process consisted of grinding up rock with lower-grade ore content, which had been passed over during the early days of mining when richer ore was at hand. The pulverized rock was then put through chemical and mechanical wash processes to extract the ore. Huge new plants, and new mines, were needed. Minnesota had been rich in iron ore, much of it located in the central and north-central parts of the state with unerring accuracy so as to miss every one of the nearby Indian reservations (which has caused the Ojibway to speculate wryly whether it was really true that the location of the ore deposits was unknown until after establishment of the reservations). The ore was to have lasted for centuries, but this prediction was made before the insatiability of world-war economies and induced consumer consumption were experienced. By the 1950s the richer ore-bearing rock was becoming scarcer or less competitive with high-grade ore from Venezuela, Quebec, and Africa.

Efficient taconite production made it desirable to locate the plants either at the mine site or at the shipping points on Lake Superior, where ore boats could use the St. Lawrence Seaway to haul the taconite pellets to Chicago and Pittsburgh. Because the taconite plants needed water, some were located right on Lake Superior. In the early 1960s science-fiction-type plants and piers were carved out of the cliffs and forests, while rail spurs led from the inland to the computerized belts and machinery, and a modern highway was carved and dynamited along the North Shore. No one then anticipated that a byproduct of these intrusions would be massive amounts of asbestos fibers in the purest, largest freshwater body in the world. Had this been anticipated, the plants might have been built inland and the finished pellets moved to the lakeshore by rail, for today the taconite plants have to truck processing residues and wastes back inland. And with inland plants, the proposed lakeshore national park might have been feasible as well. It appears to be too late now.

Andersen had risen to prominence through grit and determination, a model of early twentieth-century midwestern values. Orphaned in his teens and self-supporting, struck by polio and meningitis while a youngster, he overcame poverty and illness selling newspapers on a hard-fought corner, selling stories he had written to a newspaper, as an adult selling the products of firms. He came to head the Fuller Company with 23 plants, was elected to the state senate repeatedly, and ultimately to the governship. Concurrently he had also acquired a farm, realizing a boyhood wish; and long after his retirement from politics, at a time in life when leisure and relaxation is relished by many people, he initiated a new career which also stemmed from a boyhood wish. He bought two smalltown newspapers and became a publisher, while remaining active in philanthropic and civic work.

Andersen's administration was effective in promoting taconite development, as were his successors. While this industrial innovation was being engineered, Andersen pushed for expansion of state parks and recreation facilities, and renewed the campaign for the national park. Within weeks of taking office, invitations were issued to Park Service officials to visit Kabetogama on the grounds that the Park Service itself had deemed it a potential national-park site. In the summer of 1961 the assistant director came from Washington, accompanied by regional staff. Hella and other Minnesotans took them on a boat, hiking, and airplane tour of Kabetogama; they left impressed, indicating that the matter would be taken forward. The combination of Hella's championship of the park and Andersen's assessment of needs put new zest in the proposal for a national park. And in Andersen the conservationists had a powerful and effective organizer and advocate.

Next spring Andersen invited Park Service Director Conrad Wirth to Minnesota to dedicate a new state park at Bear Head Lake, and to tour the Kabetogama site personally. Some years before Wirth's father had helped lay out the famous Minneapolis park system, and he had taken his teen-age son canoeing up north during the time the family lived in Minneapolis. On June 27, 1962, Wirth came to see Kabetogama for himself. His hosts included not only Andersen and Hella and an entourage of state officials designed to cover forestry, recreation, and related disciplines, but also Russell Fridley, director of the Minnesota Historical Society, who knew well the area's archaeology and history; George Amidon, representing Minnesota and Ontario Paper, the largest Kabetogama landholder, whose presence and participation indicated that the big firm, although not enthusiastic about the park proposal, was being civil; and Sigurd Olson, geologist, ecologist, writer, and moral spokesman for conservation.

Olson, who was coming to be the symbol of the Quetico-Superior movement and of national ecological concern, was taking over from the aging Oberholtzer as the spearhead of border-country protection. Olson felt that the park proposal was a now-or-never matter and that within 10 years the demand for recreation lands would inflate real-estate prices beyond reasonable reach.

The group took a boat to Kettle Falls, then another through Namakan and Kabetogama on an extraordinarily beautiful day. They behaved like tourists, admiring the sights, fishing on the way, exchanging anecdotes. Among these people with diverse interests, from different disciplines emerged a consensus in the course of the trip that Kabetogama must be saved and a national park for the area be established.

What should it be called? Names were bandied about and Olson, in the same boat with Wirth, proposed *Voyageurs* "because I felt the area was part of the ancient voyageurs highway along the border," well past the point where the alternate routes joined to form the main trunk.

"That's it!" Wirth exclaimed and the group agreed.

Meeting of the minds in naming the proposed park did not preclude the members of the party from chaffing one another about their fishing skill. Wirth caught a bigger walleye than Andersen and told him, "You don't even know where the fish are in your state." It was a benign, friendly occasion and the decision to press for park establishment was firm, unanimous, and seemed quite natural. Years later, after the park had finally been established, Wirth was to comment wryly that it had set a record. It was "the one park in the national system with the longest track from first proposal to final approval."

Andersen wrote a statement in longhand announcing that the members of the group agreed that the historical, geological, and recreational values of Kabetogama justified serious study of it as a potential national park. On his return to Washington, Wirth got the wheels in motion and Park Service experts from the Omaha Regional Office and elsewhere were dispatched. A serious effort was under way.

What had to be done was a painstaking inventory of flora and fauna, of soil composition and geology, so that it could be determined what park activities and facilities would be suitable, and where. There had to be studies of the economics of a park: how many people could be expected to visit, how would they get there, where would they stay—in campgrounds, lodgings, at what location? Who owned which parcel, and what was it worth? What impact would a park have on the surrounding area economically, ecologically? What ecological impact would the surrounding area have on the park? The Canadians were inclined to private development, including mining and power-plant construction as well as the ongoing private cabin construction. What should be done about the small clusters of resorts on the southwest of Kabetogama Lake, at the end of the Ash River, and on Crane Lake? Should a park provide for more roads into the area, for massive construction of facilities, or should it stress water travel? These and other questions would have to be answered before any cost estimates could be done; and Congress, which had to approve the park, would require both answers and cost figures.

Andersen and Wirth agreed that the fact-finding was a job for both the Park Service and Minnesota. Before freezeup in 1962 the first teams were at work. But in the November elections Andersen lost, and although the new governor also favored a park for the area, the project appeared once again headed for the shelf. It did not have the drive and impetus it had when the proponents were personally involved and when it was part of a carefully constructed overall plan for the region. Andersen's strategy of keeping the park proposal separate from the plight of Quetico-Superior and the Boundary Waters Canoe Area, involving decades of dispute and hosts of coalesced proponents and opponents, had not had time to jell, he had not been in office long enough. One element of the strategy had been to avoid not only the disputes and chosen sides of the BWCA, but also the issues of logging and mining that were plaguing the Superior National Forest and BWCA: these were not permitted in a national park.

It now seemed that at most the studies and assessments would be completed and filed, as earlier ones had been, destined for footnotes in graduate papers and perhaps serving as a springboard for yet another try at establishing a park at some distant time.

7

Politics of Environmental Concern

The Park Service issued its preliminary report on the proposed park early in 1964, less than a year after Andersen had vacated the governor's office to return to private life. The findings and recommendations unequivocally favored establishing Voyageurs National Park. A few months before, the September 1963 *National Geographic* reached a national audience with an article written by Sigurd Olson describing underwater searches by skin-diving archaeologists and their massive finds of voyageur trade goods and artifacts near the proposed park area. The article ended on an upbeat, hopeful note that anticipated the Park Service conclusions and urged Congress to approve a Voyageurs National Park.

The idea of using archaeologists under water to locate artifacts of the fur trade came to E. W. Davis, inventor of the taconite extraction process, while watching scuba divers at work in Lake Superior. Surely *some* voyageur canoes must have capsized or gone down, he theorized; what had they contained? He contacted Olson, an expert on the area and the voyageur period, who agreed. They selected "suitable" places, rapids and falls that could be "shot" at some risk, and eliminated the ones that would be impossible to negotiate by canoe under any circumstance. They first concentrated on more difficult rapids, and did not find any artifacts in the dangerous currents. Subsequent efforts along the Granite River, between Gunflint and Saganaga Lakes, yielded findings beyond their highest expectations. There was a set of nested brass kettles, iron ax heads and ice chisels so necessary for winter beaver trapping, flintlock muskets, over a thousand musket balls, quantities of vermilion paint, brass buttons, thimbles, gunflint, pewter, and other goods. They dated to the 1790s, and Indian artifacts from the sites were much older: pipestems, spear points, and other evidence suggesting that voyageurs were not the only ones to tip over in treacherous waters. Indians using the customary 15-foot birchbark hunting canoes apparently had mishaps too.

In subsequent years underwater archaeology in the boundary waters developed its own technology, and quantities of broken clay pipes were found at the Ft. Charlotte site and elsewhere; many voyageurs were heavy smokers, and the clay pipes were fragile. The archaeologists have since provided detailed knowledge of several sites, but in 1963 the article created a stir. The daring, dramatic underwater search in the rapids, and the finds, made the dangerous, exciting days of the voyageurs come to life.

Olson was in a unique position to champion the park. He had personally canoed most of the 2,000 miles of the voyageurs highway from Grand Portage to the Athabasca country and beyond, and as a young man he had guided canoe parties in the Quetico-Superior country and knew it intimately. He also drew on his professional skills as geologist and ecologist. Like Oberholtzer, Olson had chosen to combine his professional life with his deep feelings for the north country. He moved to Ely in the 1920s to teach, guide, and ultimately to lecture and write, and to live his outdoor life where it suited him best. Like Oberholtzer, Olson would complain that his efforts in behalf of wilderness conservancy were too little and too late, but his stream of books and articles reached and maintained popularity and spoke to a nationwide audience. Olson was consulted by the Interior Department and the Park Service on wilderness preservation; he was influential in the Izaak Walton League, president of the Wilderness Society, active in the Sierra Club, and he served on the president's Quetico-Superior Committee.

Some national curiosity about the area and the voyageurs of the fur trade was aroused by Olson's piquant article in the *National Geographic*. It was now bolstered by the Park Service findings. Andersen's successor, Karl Rolvaag, eventually endorsed the park proposal, apparently casting about for new programs of his own before concluding that Voyageurs was the best prospect. However, there is always competition between states and interest groups for the establishment of parks, and few proposals get as far as introduction before Congress, much less passage. All signs pointed to an early demise for the Voyageurs Park in 1964 despite the affirmative response from the Park Service and the publicity. There was no constituency organized and committed to seeing the matter through. The few voices raised on its behalf, though prestigious and eloquent, were not enough.

In early 1964 the Minneapolis Chamber of Commerce appointed a tourism study committee and named a young executive, Martin Kellogg, chairman. It was a traditional move in the grooming of energetic new talent. Kellogg was to work with Lloyd Brandt, the Chamber's legislative affairs executive. The two decided to make short shrift of the project and to present concise recommendations to bolster the sagging industry. Kellogg's quest for ideas led him to Andersen, who had returned to private life but was conducting a shadow government from his offices in St. Paul, promoting the taconite referendum so essential to establishing the the new industry, and other civic and bipartisan causes.

"You're missing the main point," Andersen told Kellogg. "What the resorts and the businesses up north need is a national park that will draw thousands of people to the area."

Andersen was persuasive, appealing in turn to Kellogg's interests in the outdoors and canoeing, to the sound economics of the park proposal, to the "now or never" aspects of saving the north-country wilderness from private lakeshore development and further exploitation, and to the desirability of putting this unique area, valuable geologically and historically, in "protective custody."

"I wish I could have gotten it through when I was governor," Andersen said. "It wouldn't even hurt the paper companies. They get less than 10,000 cords a year out of the park area, and meanwhile there is a surplus of hundreds of thousands of cords in Koochiching and St. Louis Counties nearby."

Andersen had names, many names, of people who would favor a park. In International Falls there were Wayne Judy, owner of a sporting-goods store, and Judge Mark Abbott. Judy had told Hella earlier that he would be willing to organize local support for the park when the time came because he thought "the National Park service would do a better job than anyone else in preserving this area that I love so much so that our children and their children could enjoy it as I knew it and loved it."

Andersen said he would be willing to contact paper-company officials and others, if that proved necessary. But first he thought Kellogg should organize a citizens' group on behalf of Voyageurs National Park and draw into it a wide spectrum of interests from the entire state. Later it could become a national organization. And it should seek to get support for the park from each member of the Minnesota Congressional delegation, from the national conservation organizations, and from the media. Kellogg, who had come in search of ideas, left with a mission and a copy of the Park Service proposal.

Referring to the voyageur route as "America's first transcontinental highway," the report traced the history and geology of the area, and the long trail of proposals that it be made a park. The Park Service had examined the resort and vacation aspects of the area, and termed it among the best fishing grounds in the north. A proposed park would meet the existing Superior National Forest and its Boundary Waters Canoe Area at Crane Lake, and this area would be cooperatively developed by the Forest Service and the Park Service.

On one of the key questions, the Park Service findings were that the area "is large enough to include the essential land and water needed for logical administration, development and protection, and for effective interpretation and use . . . which do not conflict with basic preservation."

The significance of the area made it worthy of inclusion in the National Park System because of its "human history, the ancient rock exposures, . . . its superb wilderness scenery, the variety of plant and animal life."

To preserve this "the boat will replace the car as the primary means of transportation throughout the park as no roads are intended or needed."

There was nothing quite like it in the national park system, the report found, and Voyageurs should be added. Almost wistfully, the Park Service added that it would be "most desirable if our neighbors in Canada could institute a similar program so that management of the natural resources on both sides . . . would be comparable."

Some of the language in the proposal was colorful and enthusiastic, as though written by a Minnesotan: "The drama of the voyageurs and . . . the Indians . . . was enacted upon a land patterned by the glaciers. These . . . robbed this land of its fertile mantle and gave it to the midlands. . . . They exposed the most ancient of the earth's rocks, even the very roots of former mountains that had a billion years previously been peneplained to a rolling upland . . . carving out the present drainage. Forests . . . now cover the area. . . . Numerous animals and birds—moose, beaver, the mysterious loon . . . can be observed here. . . . The National Park Service recommends the establishment."

Flowery language notwithstanding, Kellogg and Brandt found the report convincing. They were further encouraged by Hella, and issued a strong committee report calling for passage of park legislation by Congress, which the Chamber accepted, thus setting the stage for later effective support among Twin Cities' business and professional people, and potential upstate sympathizers. Soon after, three International Falls men — Judy, Judge Abbott, and George Esslinger — met with Kellogg and Brandt. Esslinger was a guide and trapper in the Kabetogama area who specialized in raising and training sleddogs, and who had participated in special dog-sled rescue teams in Greenland and Europe during World War II. The upshot of the meeting was an agreement to organize the

Voyageurs National Park Association. Andersen suggested Judge Edwin P. Chapman, Hennepin County Municipal Court, as president. St. Paul investment manager Tom Savage was secretary, Brandt vice president, and Kellogg treasurer. The International Falls group would organize local support, and eventually there came to be chapters of the association in many communities in the state. Andersen participated personally and was influential in attracting a number of powerful and prominent personalities to the association, including Wheelock Whitney, Walter Dayton, and Charles Mayo.

Over the months that followed, the association generated a tattoo of newspaper, radio, and television coverage of the park proposal; it was a sustained campaign that did not slacken for the several years from the association's founding to the success of its initial mission. Kellogg, in retrospect, took it for granted that it had to be this way, because the campaign for the park was essentially a campaign to inform the public and obtain its support. At the same time, the association built a membership, and, through it, a basis for fund raising.

This development in citizen diplomacy paralleled events on behalf of the Quetico-Superior four decades earlier, when public interest in conservation was rallied by the organization led by Oberholtzer and his friends, and subsequently by Olson. Now both Olson and the aging Oberholtzer lent their support, as did the organizations who had valiantly fought on behalf of the Superior: the Izaak Walton League, chapters of the Audubon Society, Defenders of Wildlife, Friends of Wilderness Society, the Nature Conservancy, Sierra Club, and many others. But before these national organizations were mobilized on behalf of Voyageurs, the park proponents carefully lined up their state chapters and organizations, both political parties, labor unions, cooperatives, churches, and farm, fraternal, travel, women's, and professional groups. And the Minnesota Twins. It became a spirited, enthusiastic bandwagon carefully sparked by local support in International Falls and the media-conscious, communications-oriented Twin Citians.

Andersen drafted Rita Shemesh to help with organization and promotion. Mrs. Shemesh had impressed Brandt, Andersen, and others by her work on behalf of the taconite amendment. The wife of an anatomy instructor, medical illustrator, cartoonist, and prominent physician, Mrs. Shemesh somehow managed her household, young children, her hobby of growing orchids, and devoted virtually full time to the park.

"It was like being in a long, dark tunnel," she said. "We did not know where we would come out, or when."

Under Rita Shemesh's guidance, Voyageurs Park was continually in the news. The smallest event, such as a vote of support or endorsement by a village fraternal organization, was good for a press release. A professionally created film was made available, narrated by Sigurd Olson, showing the beauties of the area which might well be lost without park status.

Don Fraser, elected to Congress in 1962 from a Minneapolis district, was the first member of the delegation to strongly call for the park. Soon the entire delegation, representing both parties, in House and Senate, was unanimous in its support, responding to telephone calls from the inveterate Andersen and his associates in the Voyageurs National Park Association. Even Fraser, who needed no convincing or prompting to persuade him of the park proposal's merits, received several calls from Andersen and others.

When the park proposal began the difficult and uncertain course through introduction, committee hearings, public hearings, and action by the Congress, its principal champion and warrior was Congressman John Blatnik, whose district ranged from Duluth to include the bulk of the border-lakes territory. Blatnik and his assistant, James Oberstar (later to succeed to Blatnik's seat), were at the storm center of any controversy, brokering agreements and consensus between conflicting interests, and at the same time obtaining the necessary votes. It was certain to be a difficult role, for not only were there potential differences in the home district, but there was no assurance that the rest of the country would share the Minnesotans' views or those of the Park Service, or that the federal bureaucracy would support the effort.

Blatnik had a reputation for taking a long time to make up his mind on controversial issues, some felt too long, although Oberstar explained that the veteran Congressman just liked to look into all matters very thoroughly.

"Well, two terms in office should be long enough," park proponents grumbled, and pointedly sent his office copies of news stories, supportive editorials, and opinion surveys showing strong support for the park among resorters, sportsmen, and other interest groups. But Blatnik's political instincts had served him well through many years and controversial issues, and he knew that the brouhaha, when it came, would not be confined to his own district.

Tension between the Forest Service, which managed the Superior and Boundary Waters, and the Park Service, which would manage the adjoining park, had been endemic and sometimes bitter, if not openly admitted. Their roles and approaches to conservation had traditionally been different, and intramural competition for turf had been acrimonious. Gifford Pinchot more than once spoke tartly to nationwide audiences about the need for the Forest Service as a manager and producer of timber, while his counterparts in the Park Service had been known to criticize the sometimes liberal logging practices of the Forest Service. So sharp was the rivalry at times that when a Forest Service field supervisor wanted to scare more budget money out of his Washington headquarters, he would invite some Park Service friends nearby to tour the forest and then inform headquarters that the enemy was surveying the site as a possible park; the budget increase, previously denied, then materialized. When the Park Service surveyed the Kabetogama area with Civilian Conservation Corps help in the 1930s and recommended a national park *including* the Superior Forest, the screams of anguish were predictable, as was the outcome. The two organizations were once again brought into juxtaposition, or at least into close proximity and coordination. It could be a complicating factor for the legislators.

Other potential danger points were competing park proposals elsewhere in the country, the continuing conflict over logging and mining in the Superior Forest, and the role of the logging and paper industries in the proposed park area. Backus's conglomerate, Minnesota and Ontario, had indicated tolerance of the plan, if not exuberance for it; but in 1965 Minnesota and Ontario, with its local roots and history, was acquired by Boise Cascade Corporation, whose national posture and concerns might give them a different bent. Also there would be challenges from hunters and snowmobile interests. Blatnik, Oberstar, and their associates would have no easy task, so it was an advantage that the legislative process had to wait for completion of the Park Service studies, issuance of a master plan, and drafting of proposed legislation.

From 1965 until the first Blatnik bill was introduced in July 1968 the association continued to build membership, promote and publicize the park, and raise money. Celebrities rallied to the cause, including Arthur Godfrey, Charles Lindbergh, and Justice William Douglas.

But opposition to the park rallied also, seemingly sparked by the Boise Cascade acquisition of the M & O. Minnesota and Ontario had let it be known through its spokesman George Amidon that it would not oppose the park. This changed overnight, and it began to appear the Boise Cascade opposition was motivated by its ownership of a land-development subsidiary that had plans for the Kabetogama lakeshore.

Journalists talked about Boise Cascade's efforts to wine and dine them. Local supporters of the park in International Falls—particularly Wayne Judy, whose retail activities made him very vulnerable—found themselves boycotted by many people. Judge Abbott and Esslinger were not economically dependent on local trade for their livelihoods, but heard their share of criticism. Most of the resistance dealt with the loss of hunting grounds; resort operators, by and large, seemed to support the park.

Some of the differences in view were exchanged in a civil manner. After one hearing, Kendall taunted Amidon:

"I'll see you at the dedication of the park."

"I'll be there if there is one," Amidon retorted. "But I'll fight like hell to prevent that dedication."

It was not always that polite. At a meeting in International Falls called by state officials for the purpose of having National Park Service staff explain plans and answer questions, the audience was raucous and jeering as parks designer John Kawamoto sought to explain the various plans. Hella finally rose and reminded the people that the park designers were there at his invitation on behalf of the state and were entitled to courtesy. This helped a little, but not enough to suit Frank B. Hubachek, a large man who was one of Oberholtzer's close friends and supporters and sponsor of wilderness research. Hubachek roundly scolded the audience for their lack of good manners, and the rest of the meeting was orderly. Duck hunting on Black Bay was superb, and local hunters did not want to lose the area, although there were equally good hunting spots outside the proposed park.

Hunters were encouraged by the company's public position, which favored a national park in northern Minnesota so long as it was not at Kabetogama, and which promised that the company, as the major landowner of the peninsula, would develop it in such a way that there would always be hunting, picnicking, and camping. Boise Cascade held that it was the best manager of the lands, that the state was second-best, and the federal government last. This position appealed to local conservationists who also felt that the least government was the best and who opposed a national park on those grounds.

Esslinger countered this, arguing that "we have to give up something now for the future, otherwise there will be nothing left in a hundred years, we've got to protect the resources."

A Kabetogama resort operator, Earl Yates, commented tartly that "the opponents are a small but loud group from the Falls. They have never cared about Kabetogama. How did they now suddenly become our spokesmen? The park should be of great benefit to us. Most of us resorters are convinced of that. It would give our lakes . . . national stature, and bring a lot of business here. Most of the businessmen in Falls are in favor of the park." It seemed that Yates was right, because Wayne Judy was able to show on the record support for the park by the chamber, retail merchants, labor unions, and the district Democratic Farmer Labor convention. Opinion polls backed this up.

Andersen felt that many people upstate meant well but did not look ahead very far, and he knew from his days as an elected official that the politics of the northern counties tended to be fierce and bitter. Andersen had breakfast with the Boise Cascade president and pleaded for the park, but at that time the company had big dreams of resort developments in Illinois, Idaho, California, and in Minnesota. Soon after, the development bubble burst, and the firm's opposition became less spirited. Having said that the park would mean loss of jobs owing to loss of pulpwood, an argument not supported by logging statistics, the company could not publicly turn about.

Worried by the first signs of organized opposition, the association commissioned a professional polling organization to take a public-opinion survey. It was conducted in Blatnik's 8th Congressional District by Mid Continent Surveys in early 1968, and showed two-thirds expressing outright approval of a national park in the Kabetogama area, only 20 percent opposed. Eight of ten adults in the area either favored it or did not oppose it. Surveyors probed the respondents' reasons more deeply. Those in favor of the park cited (in order) its advantages: bringing in more tourists, retail, and new enterprises; preserving forests and keeping the forest area from becoming commercialized; and providing a recreational area for the people. If Blatnik had been concerned about the extent of the opposition, the survey would have put such doubts to rest. As it was, Blatnik had canoed in the north country for many years, knew its history, and cherished its values.

When the survey results were announced, Dr. Charles W. Mayo, then chariman of the Citizens Committee for Voyageurs National Park, a parallel organization to the association, said: "Very few public propositions have enjoyed such strong support in the area most affected. . . . There is very high awareness of the proposal and very high understanding of the benefits of the park, we have learned from the study."

Most state newspapers agreed editorially.

Early in 1968 the United Northern Sportsmen Club in Duluth issued a lengthy report on the park. The club had given its approval in 1964, but the controversy caused it to appoint a study committee. This group made an exhaustive study, weighed the alternatives suggested by Boise Cascade and others (including parks at Lac La Croix, Grand Portage, Itasca); it examined other options such as having no park at all, a state park, a national recreation area, a joint-county management area. The conclusion and recommendation of the study group, accepted by the club, was a very strong endorsement of the national park proposal, all alternatives having been considered in detail.

The Sportsmen Club's precise conclusions were indicative of the informed public debate, and prescient in that they spelled out the structure and compromises of the legislation in its final form, approved almost two years later—with the exception of hunting (which the club thought should be allowed in the park, but which was not to be).

Blatnik introduced the bill in July 1968, knowing it was likely to be swallowed up by the turmoil of a presidential election year, but hoping it would serve at least as an entering wedge. The association and its companion Citizens Committee, joined now by scores of other organizations and a still-growing roster of prominent Minnesotans, conducted workshops and seminars at Rainy Lake Lodge near International Falls, tours of the proposed park, visits at the Kettle Falls Hotel, and boat trips on Rainy and Kabetogama Lakes. Delegates to such seminars paid their own way, including fare for air trips over the peninsula.

Opposition to the park now changed its line, calling for development as a "multiple use" area where logging, hunting, and mechanized travel would coexist with activities like camping and hiking. Boise Cascade pointed to its protection of the shoreline timber and to the picnic and camping areas established by the firm at its own expense. Park advocates countered that these improvements were few and of small consequence, and dependent on company initiatives which could change at any time; to the park proponents, "multiple use" became a synonym for timber companies running rampant, until Judge Chapman pointed out that "the park was a form of multiple use." He spoke to a group of foresters, reminding them that former U.S. Forest Service Chief Richard McCardle had defined multiple use as a "coordination of various uses, not on each acre, but on large blocks of land in a way designed to get the optimum combination of uses for the benefit of the public." Chapman then pointed to the complementary roles of Voyageurs and the Superior Forest, a line of reasoning that found wide acceptance.

Andersen usually worked quietly, staying in touch with old friends and acquaintances in the state legislature, the state capitol, and Washington, exercising his powers of persuasion and salesmanship. But now he conceived a bold public-relations venture, inviting Charles Lindbergh to endorse Voyageurs Park. The famous flier was a Minnesota native; his avid support of parklands and conservation was well known, his national reputation could win the venture needed publicity and acceptance. Lindbergh wrote back kindly, explaining he never endorsed anything he had no personal knowledge of, however worthy, but he might be willing to do so once he had seen the place. This seemed to be the end of the matter, since Lindbergh was then abroad and he did not mention plans of coming to Minnesota. Unexpectedly a few weeks later, Andersen received a call from Historical Society Director Russell Fridley, a friend of both Lindbergh and Andersen, announcing that Lindbergh would arrive that day, would be willing to meet with park proponents, would go to see the park, but would allow no newspaper interviews or pictures, much less television. Lindbergh's proverbial shyness and quest for anonymity ran counter to Andersen's wishes, but he hurriedly set about to make transportation arrangements at Minneapolis, and for air and boat facilities at International Falls. Lindbergh insisted that no one at Falls be told who was renting the sea plane and the boat. His appearance, therefore, was a surprise to airport manager Francis Einerson, and Esslinger, who was on hand to guide the party.

Lindbergh piloted the plane over the Kabetogama Peninsula with Andersen alongside in the two-seater, the diffident aviator and the ebullient promoter striking up a warm friendship. Lindbergh, eager to see a moose, asked Andersen if he had ever piloted a plane.

"No, and I doubt I'd care to," he answered.

"Nothing to it. You just take hold of this stick and move it back and forth, left or right, up or down, depending on where you want to go. Here, take over so I can look for a moose. And remember I'm right here."

Andersen's wish to survive struggled with his hopes for the park, and the park won; he took the stick in his clammy hands and held on for dear life. Lindbergh did not see a moose, Andersen did not crash the plane, and they landed safely.

Back in the Twin Cities Lindbergh agreed to a press conference under his conditions. Reporters were to be invited, but not told in advance who would be at Andersen's home (those who came obtained an unusual story, those who did not bemoaned their luck). Furthermore, the interview would take the form of a conversation between Lindbergh and Andersen, which the reporters could quote, but no questions would be allowed. It was definitely not the way Andersen approached press relations, but he respected Lindbergh's wishes and had, by now, become captivated by his guest's gentle and thoughtful approach to life.

"The area is so beautiful and extraordinary," Lindbergh wrote after the visit, "that it seems to me it would be a tragedy to miss the (probably never to return) opportunity of establishing it as a national park." He followed this with a letter to the House Committee on Interior and Insular Affairs the next year, when hearings were to be held on Voyageurs Park legislation: "It would make one of the world's great . . . national parks. It is one of the most beautiful and attractive areas I have seen."

Lindbergh's belief was that "without the balance of the wilderness, . . . a key part of the value of life would be lost. . . . Our lands, our waters, the resources of our world are not just owned outright by us but held in trust for the short periods of our lifetimes. To consume and to despoil them in one extravagant splurge would be a crime against our children and their children." The concept of man as trustee and guardian in relationship to the land was not original with Lindbergh, but his utterance in support of Voyageurs lent weight and national recognition.

In April 1969 Blatnik reintroduced the legislation on behalf of the entire Minnesota delegation; on the Senate side Walter Mondale and Eugene McCarthy introduced the companion bill. Blatnik had a surprise; having taken four to five years before committing himself to the park proposal, he now was adamant that if there was to be a park, it had to go all the way to Crane Lake. This meant a transfer of lands from the Superior Forest to the Park Service. Blatnik was convinced that the park, thus encompassing three access routes instead of two, would be available to more people, and that it would make a more integral whole, one that would have much more to offer the visitor. Park advocates were horror-struck: they anticipated that the powerful Forest Service would muster opposition, that the addition would complicate the legislative process. But they failed to realize how much power Blatnik had, now that he was slated to head the Public Works Committee. Some officials in the Forest Service muttered that not only was

Blatnik motivated to make the proposed park as good as possible, but he was affording himself the opportunity of chastising them for their past intransigence. However, the Forest Service was in no position, nor mood, to take on the chairman of the Public Works Committee. Many wheels began to turn as the Park Service, environmental and conservation organizations, and the association concentrated their efforts. At the last moment it seemed the bill would be held over to the next session; Congressman Aspinall, powerful and domineering chairman of the House Interior Committee, felt it was too late in the session and he would not be able to work it in. Blatnik good-humoredly reminded Aspinall that he had less seniority (by eleven months) and that Blatnik had been thinking about bumping him and taking over the Interior Committee himself. On second thought, Blatnik added, it was more fun to chair the Public Works Committee (which had to act on bills in which Aspinall had an interest). Aspinall smiled wryly and put the bill on the agenda for that session.

It was only one of many obstacles, and Blatnik, often working through Oberstar, had to muscle his way through the legislative labyrinth. Congressman McClure, thought by some observers to be favorable to his Idaho constituency of timber companies (including Boise Cascade), was not making life easy for the proposal. Congressman Udall, although favorable, did not share Blatnik's sense of urgency.

Hearings were held at International Falls in August 1969 and dispelled any doubts that Blatnik and others might have had about public sentiment. Park proponents and letters of endorsement from organizations greatly outnumbered the opposition. It only remained for the main hearings to be held in Washington before the matter would come to a vote, and these were finally scheduled for the early summer of 1970.

The House hearings were critical for the park proposal, and to the dismay of pro-park witnesses waiting to testify, Minnesota Governor Harold LeVander, who had succeeded Rolvaag, was plumping for a recreation area where hunting would be allowed. He was followed to the witness stand by Andersen, whose strong testimony, backed by literally thousands of endorsements and letters of support from state officials, national and state conservation organizations, and private citizens proved persuasive. Boise Cascade's presentation of itself as the best manager of the area was riddled by detailed questions from committee members: How many campgrounds would there be? Facilities for how many people? How many picnic tables, fireplaces, trails? There were only a few, a token development, and the company appeared, by its stance, to be devious. Some suggested the firm was intending to use the lakeshore for real-estate development.

More dispute and emotion was aroused by the issue of hunting in the park. It was generally known that the Park Service opposed hunting in its parks, as it did logging and mining. Although other issues had been ironed out in countless meetings between Blatnik's staff, the Park Service, and others, by the time of the hearings three or four bones of contention remained — all participants well aware of what they were and that they would be aired. Blatnik knew hunting would be one of them, and the length of time that the Kettle Falls and other facilities could be operated by the present owners would also be in contention. During the preliminary skirmishing, Park Service lawyers jokingly offered Blatnik's staff a trade: a park with no hunting or a 40-acre monument with all the hunting they wanted. The lawyers knew the sentiment of the Congressional committee members, who offered a similar trade when Minnesota state officials pleaded for continued hunting during the hearings. Having a national park was more important than being allowed to hunt.

Congressman Fraser, testifying for the park, noted the paucity of water-based parkland in the east North-Central states. Only the Mid-Atlantic states had fewer per capita acres of inland water surface within easy access of population centers. "National population trends indicate that it is important to set aside a . . . preserve now." Noting that the North-Central states had been lowest in population growth in 1960, the trend had changed from 1965 to 1968, Fraser urged "the wisdom of setting aside . . . land to meet the region's growing recreational needs."

Fraser voiced concern about "the problems of environmental degradation. . . . Our environmental problems nationally make[s] it imperative that we take adequate steps now to preserve for posterity those few areas of our country which still remain environmentally pure. The land . . . [of] this proposed park is one of those few remaining areas."

It all looked promising, the end was in sight. The House Committee favored Voyageurs National Park on the expanded basis, reaching from Black Bay to Crane Lake, as a full-fledged park without logging, mining, or hunting; however, there would be a compromise that allowed some snowmobile and motorboat use. Motorboats had to be permitted because the lakes were so large, and the snowmobile enabling language was a gesture toward the sportsmen. Park proponents were not happy about the compromise, but bowed to it as a political necessity. Andersen paid protocol visits on the Senate side, planning to return to Minnesota, and found out to his shock and chagrin that nothing had been done there, and that there were no serious prospects for consideration of Voyageurs.

He received a rapid indoctrination to Washington politics. Apparently Boise Cascade had been given to understand that whatever happened to the park lesiglation on the House side, it would never come to a vote in the Senate. This explained why the company had not made more of a fight before the House committee, why Kendall, prepared with a briefcase of evidence of environmental sins committed by Boise Cascade, never had to use his "ammunition."

Andersen, helped by Sigurd Olson, obtained a conference with Senator Henry Jackson and persuaded him of the importance and value of the Voyageurs proposal, noting the extent of state and public support for the park. Jackson, miffed that the issue had been misrepresented to him, vowed he would make up for it and press for consideration during the current session. Blatnik and Oberstar worked with their committee staff counterparts on the Senate side. In the peculiar language of Washington, Blatnik thanked key senators for considering the Voyageurs proposal and let it be known he would remember their kind assistance when *their* bills came over to the House side and before *his* committee.

Ten years after the park legislation was passed, Washington officials still recalled the onslaught of the Minnesotans and remembered some of the lobbyists by name. Officials and staff members of every major, and minor, park, recreation, conservation, and out-

doors organization had vivid recollections, as did the travel, automobile, veterans', fraternal, and labor organizations. For instance,
the national AFL-CIO was reminded of its interest in the availability of economical leisure and recreational activities for its
members—activities which a major Lake States park would provide in an area of the country short on such facilities at the time.
David K. Roe of the Minnesota AFL-CIO was an active park supporter. The American Legion was reminded that it had passed a
number of resolutions at national conventions calling for the International Peace Memorial Forest and that the Voyageurs Park was a
step in that direction.

Pervasive and persistent, Andersen had used his contacts, skills,
and enthusiastic salesmanship in Washington and in Minnesota,
backed up by the association and its chapters and the Citizens
Committee. The Minnesota Legislature's Outdoor Recreation Resources Commission issued an extensive report in 1965 endorsing
the park, and another report in 1967, furnishing statistical and fac-
tual economic and environmental ammunition. Organizations
passed resolutions and went on record in support of the park. The
association placed advertisements, prepared and disseminated bro-
chures, question-and-answer publications, and a color movie that
was shown throughout the state wherever church, social, fraternal,
or other groups wanted to see it (during two months of 1968 the
film was shown at 37 group meetings).

The bill passed the House in October 1970, the Senate in De-
cember. A conference committee negotiated language differences,
which both bodies accepted, and it was signed by the president
January 8, 1971. Almost 80 years had passed since the Minnesota
legislature had petitioned the federal government for a national
park in the border-lakes country.

The fate of Voyageurs Park to set longevity records did not end.
The law establishing the park required that Minnesota would turn
over its lands within the park boundaries to the United States.
Minnesota's Commissioner of Natural Resources, Robert Herbst,
promptly drafted the enabling act, which was quickly passed by
the state legislature, whereupon a taxpayer suit sought to block
the transfer. By the time this case percolated through the court
system and was dismissed, failing finally before the U.S. Supreme

Court, more time had passed. Formal establishment did not take place until April 1975. In June 1971 the Park Service had started things moving by assigning the park's first superintendent, Myrl Brooks, although he was titled "project manager."

Brooks, a biologist, was an interesting choice to start the park. He had worked his way up as ranger and chief ranger in assignments at Blue Ridge, Acadia, and Big Bend Parks. At Theodore Roosevelt he was chief of interpretation and resource management. Promoted to the National Park Service Washington headquarters, Brooks was assigned to master planning and legislative activities. The Park Service obviously wanted one of its best and most widely experienced men to head the establishment of the new park. A quiet man with a deep love of the outdoors, Brooks was an amateur sculptor, a Korean war veteran who had served in World War II as well, and a Rotarian, who brought his family to International Falls and settled in.

The proclivity to go to court did not end with the effort to stop the state from transferring its lands. Other actions sought to exclude duck-hunting areas from the park boundary and halt enforcement of federal regulations on the waters. Oddly enough, some staunch park supporters waffled on the hunting and water issues, including yet another Minnesota governor, Wendell Anderson, and Resources Commissioner Herbst. Local legislator Irv Anderson, a park supporter, also wavered on the issue and prevailed on his colleagues in the state capitol to legislate a Citizens Committee to advise park and state officials. For a time it appeared that the wilderness was a paradise for attorneys. Undaunted by the litigious Minnesotans, Brooks set up an office in International Falls, began the painstaking job of land acquisition, master planning for development and use of the park, and patiently establishing a working relationship with state and local officials and citizens' groups, much as the association had done.

The Voyageurs National Park Association and its local chapters decided to stay in business, issuing regular newsletters, building membership, and doggedly fighting for the park's quality. It was a good thing, because Brooks repeatedly warned that "there are chapters yet to be written about this embattled wilderness and the fight to preserve it for future generations. The continuing efforts of those who have fought so long and so hard are needed to insure that the present reality of a true national park does not fade away."

By 1977 the Park Service had augmented Brooks's skeleton staff with rangers and naturalists. Trails and camping facilities were in use. The nation's 36th national park was drawing visitors from all over the country, in winter as well as summer, for cross-country skiers and snowshoe hikers were coming to enjoy this unique place. Brooks was superintendent, no longer "project manager" once Voyageurs had been formally dedicated. Most of the private lands including the Boise Cascade holdings had been purchased, and Voyageurs was truly launched from dream to reality.

After seven years at Voyageurs, Brooks was transferred to another national park in the fall of 1978, leaving the project well under way. He had been the target of occasional sniping from park opponents to the very end of his assignment. A few local and some Washington politicians were still holding out futile promises of hunting in the park, knowing this could never be, and playing election-year politics with the park. Even Park Service and Department of Interior officials in Washington were not always supportive of their field staff and, some observers felt, of Brooks when these political games were played. As Brooks left International Falls his new friends and neighbors there regretted his departure.

It was just time to move on, Brooks smiled. He had given much of himself to get it started, and it was now in a new and different phase. Time for someone else, for new blood, for fresh leadership and management to face the different sets of challenges.

Brooks was replaced by Tom Ritter, formerly superintendent at Glacier Bay National Monument. And although the park, under Ritter's direction, would move into a new phase of management and development, it was clear that the parochial interests of hunters and snowmobilers who had harassed Brooks had not left with him, and would bedevil Ritter if he took a firm position for protecting the environmental integrity of the parklands. The Park Service in Washington would not always give the field staff strong, prompt support. Like most government at all levels, it is at times more politically sensitive to its opponents than its proponents.

8

Ecosystems of a Wilderness Park

Ecosystems are like intimate human relationships: the components need and nourish each other while demanding independence and space; changes in one bring about changes in the other, there are phases and cycles, the changes tuned to time; and there are constants represented by the life processes that make it possible for the systems to flourish in different forms when trauma disrupts or removes a component. Just as human relationships mature over years, so do ecosystem communities over a longer period. A big tree forest, for example, comes into being over several centuries.

The stage of progress of the forest determines the species of animals that thrive in it—elk, deer, caribou, or none. They, in turn, affect the presence and number of wolf, lynx, fox, and smaller creatures. The webwork chains of life, and of food, function in aquatic communities as they do in shoreland and upland life; in the intricate worlds of insects and plants, of lichens and mosses, reptiles and birds. Nature is orderly only by its own standards of life processes, not by man's; consequently, no one patch of park completely and accurately represents any one ecological community. There are always exceptions: a variety of tree that shouldn't be there, flowers and mosses customarily found elsewhere, a deer pulling up and eating water plants while a moose is browsing brush.

The broad belts identifying ecological communities in the world range from equatorial forest to subarctic tundra. Voyageurs Park falls in the *taiga*, the circumpolar conifer belt girdling the high latitudes of Europe, Asia, and North America. Leafy trees are also found, for poplar (aspen) and birch come early in the succession sequence of the forest. Birch can supplant mature pine, unless fire occurs giving the mature pine an advantage. Periodic fires help to maintain the pine community against hardwood encroachment, except (this word if not coined by ecologists should have been) where browsing animals . . . or climate . . . or soil . . . White and red pine must reach the size where the bark is thick enough so that the trees are not killed by fire. Pine will eventually dominate aspen. After this occurs, ground fires help ensure that there will be succeeding generations of pine.

Naturalists estimate that in the Voyageurs area, scoured by the glaciers and then covered by Lake Agassiz, it required less than a thousand years — perhaps 600 or 700 — for the pine forests to come into being, much as the voyageurs found them: swampland spruce, patches of aspen, maple, and birch, basswood and ash in lowland spots. Periodic fires tended to help the pine regenerate and reseed; these fires lacked the high-intensity fuel of slashings residual from logging, and tended to hold down brush and competing species without depleting the slowly accumulating soil. Some of the fires were set by Indians and had just this result.

Today's prevalent tree species is the aspen. A far second are red (Norway) pine and white pine; then in order come spruce, jackpine, ash, shrubs, black spruce, paper birch, and white cedar. Mature red and white pine forests were widespread at the time of the voyageurs. Normal life expectancy for red pine is 200 to 300 years and somewhat longer for white pine, producing an imposing forest of trees over a hundred feet tall and two to three feet in diameter. Red pine are especially spectacular because they naturally shed their lower branches in a forest stand and are straight-trunked and towering. Today the pines are not reproducing well. An ecosystems analysis was conducted by the University of Minnesota School of Forestry in 1973 for the Park Service. It warns that the native pines are "endangered in the long run." There are plenty of seedlings, but they die young, unable to compete with the other growth on the thin soil and unaided by fires that, if present, would suppress their competitors.

Hardwoods now enjoy a 3 to 1 superiority over pine, and without human intervention the park forests of the near future will be predominantly aspen and birch. A few patches of old pine can be found in the park, which make it possible to project what much of the area looked like 75 years ago, when most of the logging took place.

The entire plant community in the parklands, from marsh to meadow to upland, is remarkably rich in the variety of grasses, flowers, shrubs, and trees. Officially there are no endangered species, but the classification of grasses, wild flowers and plants and the determination of what is in danger of extinction is not as advanced for flora as it is for the animal world. We do know there are rarities, some scarce anywhere, others scarce in the park area. These include jack-in-the-pulpit, high-bush cranberries, small purple-fringed orchis and several other varieties of orchids, climbing bittersweet, wild black currant, frost grape, and a number of others. The creation of park facilities will not destroy anything unique; and planners and naturalists know the value of having a wide variety of interesting species close to development areas and will weigh the impact of any development in this context.

The bird population of the area presents a paradise for bird-watchers and photographers. There are over 100 varieties. Year-round residents include grosbeaks, nuthatches, creepers, pileated woodpeckers, chickadees; seasonal visitors fall into two classes—

those that come from the arctic during the winter, such as snow buntings and snowy owls, and those that choose temperate, southern winters, such as the geese, swan, and waterfowl who migrate over the park, and the more regular southerners who nest in the park. The latter include bald eagles, osprey, several types of hawks, warblers, songbirds, flycatchers, and finches. The most spectacular park "regulars" are the eagles, ospreys, and pileated woodpeckers, who still find safety and healthy breeding grounds, and the loon, Minnesota's protected state bird, whose haunting cries and storm warnings have come to symbolize the north country for many of its devotees. Among the unusual and startling sights in the park is the loon's courtship or territorial dance, which sends the bird skittering, literally dancing, across the water surface as it flaps its large wings. The only major changes known to have occurred in the bird population during postglacial times are the growing scarcity of spruce grouse (protected in Minnesota and Ontario, while ruffed grouse are a hunted game bird), and the extinction of the passenger pigeon (which probably was not in the area in great numbers). The presence of birds, as well as their numbers and diet, influence seed dissemination, insect control, and the balance of aquatic communities. This is a factor in decisions park planners make about locations for facilities and activities. Disrupting too many nesting or feeding sites sends shock waves throughout the larger community. Great blue herons and double-crested cormorants do more than fulfill a visitor's desire to observe picturesque birds; they are an integral part of the food chains and population control, and of the state of health of the environment.

If one wishes to, the ecosystem can be viewed in evolutionary sequence from geological origins through lakebottom and water composition, to marine life, aquatic shorelife, and so on in a giant arc that ultimately becomes a circle, leading through the food chains and relationships back to the soil, a pattern comparable to the Indian spiritual concept of the circle of life.

Kabetogama and Rainy Lakes contain at least 24 species of fish and important spawning grounds for walleye pike, a favorite of sports fishermen. There are over 30 species of aquatic plants. The aquatic community, ranging from lakebottom soils and organisms through plants, crustacea, insects, mollusks, and worms, has been studied and tested repeatedly throughout the park. The lakes are remarkably unpolluted, by all standards, such as level of dissolved oxygen near the bottom and presence of pollution-sensitive insects and their larvae. A considerable and necessary amount of organic matter has built up on the lakebottoms since the glaciers scoured the countryside and gouged out the lakebeds, and these organic deposits (which contain a record of lake history) are a working ingredient of the healthy marine metabolism. This is comparable to undisturbed nesting areas on land; to unpolluted air and the osmotic/oxygenation processes, to the relationships between land animals and land plantlife. The lakebottom sediments, an essential component of the aquatic community, are a time bomb when dredging (for marinas or to change water flowages) and dam construction or destruction is contemplated. If they are violently stirred and suspended in water, they do not settle down again quickly, which changes the chemistry, chemical processes, and metabolism of the environment.

Northern lakes are particularly sensitive to disruptions in the processes that determine oxygen levels, because the lakes freeze over. Atop the thick ice is a blanket of snow. Deprived of light, most aquatic plants die and, as they decompose, use oxygen. In small lakes or shallow bays, this can deprive fish of needed oxygen (there being virtually none available from the air because of the ice), and a winterkill of fish can result. In instances where raw or even treated sewage is dumped in water, a rush of growth results; when the lake is frozen over, such growth dies and in dying consumes oxygen, resulting in oxygen depletion. This is only one example of disrupting a healthy balance. It does not take long as was once thought to despoil a healthy environment. Lake Superior was the largest clean, sweetwater body in the world until 15 years of taconite production introduced so much abestos fiber into the water that it would take generations for the foreign matter to disappear to the lakebottom and embed in the sediments there, if taconite tailings were no longer dumped into the lake.

Throughout the park, water quality is reasonably good. There are variations owing to depth of water, amount of shore sheltering, flowage and current, and type of lakebottom; but the variations are all in the normal range, and none of the lakes can be considered polluted. However, all areas in the park are sensitive, and some have a low or a zero-level tolerance for development. It is too late to gauge the damage done by construction of the International Falls and Kettle Falls dams between 1905 and 1913; these raised the lake levels and flooded considerable upland. Subsequently there were fluctuations in water levels to satisfy flowage for power production. Such fluctuations are devastating to wild rice and seriously interfere with the spring run of spawning fish. The International Joint Commission has stopped fluctuations in Rainy Lake levels for 15 days when the ice goes out in spring to facilitate the walleye run. However, one of the results of the two dams, aside from litigation and accusations, was to galvanize the environmentalists of the 1920s into action to stop similar dam construtction elsewhere in the border lakes.

Usually the last killing frost of winter occurs around May 26 and the first about September 6. This makes for a growing season of a little over 100 days. The long winter is not a time-out, a break, in the cycle of life; large amounts of nitrogen, the essential protein ingredient, are introduced into earth and water by snow, a counterpart to the photosynthesis of summer.

Life-styles of fauna, as well as flora, change with the seasons. Only a few species truly hibernate; many slow down and become less active. The park's bears sleep it off and gestate, as do skunks; raccoons, beavers, and otters slow down. Warm sun beating on the ice during the waning winter may give a false alarm to a muskrat or even to a bear. Winter is a time for heavier pelts and different feeding habits, for some it is a time for different games, the young fox sliding and sledding in the snow. With much vegetation stripped, it is probably the best time for humans to see and observe the animals.

The dry winter air tends to be dominated by the polar air masses, as the summer is by air from the Gulf of Mexico. The average snowfall accumulates to about 60 inches, the range from very little to 160. The total precipitation averages less than 30 inches (it takes about 10 inches of snow to make up an inch of rain), and nearly half the moisture comes in June, July, and August. The effect of one or two dry years is felt quickly in the ecosystem, and results of drought are prolonged. It is yet another factor contributing to the fragility of the ecosystem, a factor more significant than the temperature ranges (from −53 or colder to 106 above) and the length of the winter.

Spring and summer arrive with a sudden rush and intensity, as in the arctic, and in some years with a raging lushness. They bring warm days and cool nights, followed by an incomparable autumn of thousands of migrating birds, cool and sometimes frosty nights; of wild-rice harvest and wild grapes, and rutting moose and deer. An incredible variety of wild berries and fruits has been ripening since midsummer and into the late fall, including blueberries, juneberries, pin and choke cherries, high- and low-bush cranberries, lingenberries, raspberries, blackberries, and thimbleberries. There is a wide variety of mushrooms. The availability of wild fruits and foods, particularly wild rice, was a major factor in the early Indians becoming first seasonal and then permanent settlers of the area soon after the disappearance of Lake Agassiz. It had been the pattern of early Indians throughout North America to turn to small game and agricultural pursuits as the big game they had followed into the continent disappeared.

As the richness of autumn gives way to the cold, huge flocks of migrating birds fly over and sometimes stop to feed and rest. They include Canada and snow geese, many kinds of ducks, hawks and warblers; they are joined by the park's summerers. Then come the long, quiet months punctuated by explosions of shrinking and expanding ice in the lakes, when humans can snowshoe, ski, or go ice fishing in backcountry which is otherwise inaccessible. It is also a time when snowmobiles can carom over the lake ice and countryside, but that is an issue of environmental impact of considerable proportions, particularly as it affects the larger animal population.

All creatures require terrain for food, reproduction, and safety; they also require territory. The park's animal population is not dense (with the possible exception of white-tailed deer), but it is varied and has been since Lake Agassiz disappeared. Before the last glacier (there were several episodes of glaciation) the park terrain probably hosted some of the now extinct species such as mastodon, woolly mammoth, giant beaver, giant bison (precursor of today's buffalo), and wild dog. We cannot be sure which of these, and which prehistoric people, were in the area before the last glacier. Since then it became, and still is, a breeding and living habitat for wolf, moose, bear, deer, lynx, fox, badger, weasel, snowshoe hare, muskrat, porcupine, mink, coyote, and many types of rodents. Fisher and marten are scarce, and the wolverine seems to have been driven out, as have the elk and the caribou.

The existence of this wildlife, in its desirable variety, is as fragile as much else in the environmental community. For example, moose are natural inhabitants of such an area and complement and contribute to the plant and animal communities. Yet on the entire Kabetogama Peninsula there are probably fewer than a dozen; a recent airplane survey revealed six. Studies by naturalists and various ecosystems analyses suggest that the elimination of cabins and resorts from the park, and thoughtful management, will enable wildlife numbers and varieties to expand slightly, and that the animal population and available food will keep each other's numbers in check. The classic experiment illustrating this (and there have now been many studies and experiments) was conducted by the climate and the ecosystems of Isle Royale beginning over 50 years ago.

Isle Royale is about 25 miles offshore from Grand Portage in Lake Superior. It is hilly and large—12 miles by 45—and was mined for copper by Indians for several thousand years. During an unusually cold winter early in this century, parts of Lake Superior froze and a few moose crossed the ice from the mainland to Isle Royale and rapidly built up a large population, to the point where the food supply was depleted. Some years later wolves crossed over to the island.

Wolf predation on sick and weak moose has kept the moose population within the bounds of the food supply without serious damage to the vegetation. Healthy moose are hard to catch, and the number of degenerative and sick or weak moose determines the size of the wolf pack. Plant community, moose, and wolves have constituted a balanced, interlocked relationship, a stable triumvirate for half a century. Isle Royale is a National Park, and its managers have seen to it that this healthy relationship is not disturbed by humans (who need no protection, since not trees, moose, nor wolves have been known to harm people).

From the early planning stages of Voyageurs National Park, thought was given to reintroducing two species that were important members of the community but were driven out at the turn of the century: the elk, or wapiti, and the woodland caribou. Both inhabited the area in significant numbers, and the difficulty of bringing them back illustrates the paradox of trying to undo environmental damage. As with a household, it is more work to clean up the mess than it would have been to prevent it in the first place.

Elk populated most of the continental United States until driven back by settlers, fences, and domestic-range animals. Early labor gangs were fed elk meat provided by hunters, and hides as well as carcasses were in demand. Entire herds were killed for the two canine teeth, or tusks, that brought up to $75 a pair. As late as 1893, when elk were becoming scarce, part of the once huge herd, then down to 1,000, was trapped in deep snow and clubbed and shot to death by settlers near Steamboat Springs, Colorado. The Minnesota elk bands lasted longer than most because the north country was not intensively exploited until about 1900. In the 1820s, large herds of elk and buffalo were seen north of St. Cloud; in 1871, a single elk was seen near Albert Lea in southern Minnesota, was chased and shot to death across the Iowa border. By the 1890s the remaining elk were in the far north of the state, and by 1917 the last were thought to have been seen near Lake of the Woods, until yet another sighting in the Northwest Angle of the same lake in 1932 (these were probably animals drifting from Manitoba).

In 1913 the state appropriated money to establish an elk herd at Itasca State Park. Ultimately 70 animals were shipped from Jackson Hole, Wyoming, and put in an enclosure at Itasca. The trapping and transportation (before the advent of tranquilizers and helicopters) took their toll, and soon only 13 animals were left. They finally began to reproduce. Some were released in the Superior National Forest but failed to take hold; a few escaped; still others were released at Itasca but failed to survive. The remainder, in a desperation move, were taken to the vast marsh and brush country of northwestern Beltrami County, not too far from Lake of the Woods, and released in 1935. There the elk began to take hold and reproduce, until they discovered the succulence of haystacks on farms at the edge of the peatbog country and farmers rediscovered the succulence of elk, as did other poachers. The elk have held their own, occasional strays being sighted up to 200 miles away from their range. But the existence of the small herd is still precarious, and despite the vastness of the territory there are probably fewer than 30 animals left after a high of nearly 70 in 1946. It is questionable whether elk can be successfully re-introduced in their former grounds in Voyageurs National Park, although the experience in Beltrami County and successes in Michigan and elsewhere could prove helpful.

Mature elk weigh about 600 to 700 pounds, which makes them considerably larger than their cousins, the woodland caribou, which once were common in northern Minnesota. The last known remnant of the caribou herd lingered until the 1940s in the same bog country that harbors the remaining elk. This poorly drained Agassiz basin, about 100 miles by 50, with its scattered spruce islands, was their last refuge in the state, even though the territory is larger than the better-known Dismal Swamp of Virginia or Florida's Okeefenokee. Woodland caribou roam in small bands and ordinarily do not migrate like the more northern barren-ground, or Barrens caribou.

Caribou were among the earliest arrivals after the glaciers along with mammoth, mastodon and giant bison, according to archaeological findings in central Minnesota. They provided a staple food for Indians in the border-lakes forests. The caribou population in Minnesota was in the thousands until settlers discovered what the Indians had known, that caribou meat was tasty. The herd declined quickly, and the scattered sightings diminished during the 1920s and 1930s, when a few animals were believed to be alive in the bog country, and a few others around the Superior National Forest and Rainy Lake.

A major effort was begun in 1932 by setting aside 480,000 acres of bog country, the Red Lake Wildlife Refuge, for the caribou. But repeated forest and peat fires during drought years, and poaching, hastened the extermination. State conservation officials conducted painstaking studies of caribou feeding and habitat needs, then obtained woodland caribou stock with the help of Canadian and Hudson's Bay Company stock. The animals were placed in the bog and forest area of the Red Lake Refuge and in the Pine Island State Forest, both within less than 100 miles of Voyageurs Park. Despite considerable sustained effort the herds did not take hold. So far as anyone knows, none have survived. Rarely strays come in from Canada, where they are rigorously protected.

It appears that bringing caribou back to the Voyageurs Park will be difficult, although food supply and habitat are favorable and will be increasingly so over the years. Perhaps caribou, which lend themselves to domestication though elk do not, can be brought back through captivity; we could employ Laplanders to show us how to do it.

The ecosystems of Voyageurs Park are varied, reasonably harmonious, and viable. Like so many delicate relationships, they have innate strength and resilience as well as vulnerability. The ecosystems of the park have coped with fire and climate change which, for a few thousand years, brought the prairies close to International Falls; when the prairie ecosystems receded, so did the buffalo, both giving way to returning *taiga*. The park's ecosystems survived the fur trade, which almost wiped out beaver and other fur-bearers; coped with logging, although this intrusion brought about major changes; and accommodated Edward Backus's dams. Humans, active participants in the ecosystems, have been continuously present for 10,000 years. So perhaps a few more millennia of harmonious coexistence are possible.

In the process of recuperating from the encroachments of humans, the ecosystems of the park are undergoing one change that could produce substantial shock waves. The end of logging in the area has resulted in a gradually maturing forest. This, in turn, means less browse for white-tailed deer, whose numbers are already diminishing. Eventually the deer herd could become very small. In an entirely natural setting, caribou and elk would move in as deer move out. This keeps the major relationships in balance, because the principal predators, wolves, can feed on elk and caribou instead of deer. Many animals depend on wolf kills for their food supply: ravens, vultures, foxes, coyotes, and countless smaller animals. Since there are no elk and caribou and the deer population is declining, this could lead to a drastic population drop in wolves, which, in turn, would lead to declines in the other populations. Park biologists are aware of this development. They know that, left entirely to itself, nature can do quite well. But when an area is a wilderness enclave in an industrial society, the ecosystems require not only respect and care, but occasional help.

9

Planning a Park

You can't put nature on an agricultural model, as the many people involved in the plans for converting Kabetogama Peninsula and the parklands into Voyageurs National Park were well aware. A wilderness park is far more complex than the nurture of one or several crops, even trees. Take just one species, moose, as an example. They are natural inhabitants, valuable because they interest visitors and control plant growth. Moose are not numerous —the herd should be bigger; their scarcity further delimits the wolf population—wolves are hardpressed by hunting and trapping in Canada and by illegal hunting and trapping in America. Since fox, coyotes, ravens, martens, and others depend on wolf kills for *their* food, the matter of the moose population becomes far more intricate than simply one of numbers. Even on Isle Royale, where control conditions are simpler because the environmental management of the surrounding area is not a factor, the moose population is a major concern for the park management. The number of moose is primarily controlled by available vegetation, their health by wolf depredation on the sick and weak. Wolves, in turn, practice their own modes of birth control in accord with *their* food supply, strictly managing mating through an effective social system. Under these seemingly ideal conditions, there are problems nevertheless. Moose are affecting the vegetation, eliminating some species almost entirely (such as yew), and there are long-term cycles in the moose population, perhaps significantly affected by fire. After a natural fire caused by lightning, there is a rush of vegetation growth that provides a feast for the moose. It can get very complicated. Should one allow fires? Under what circumstances and where? Should one enhance moose breeding and feeding grounds? To what extent and in which areas, at what cost to human use? And moose is but one example, perhaps not even the most significant.

Early American parks were wilderness areas set aside in their undeveloped condition. Under the impact of population growth and increased park use, the wilderness areas began to suffer. With 3 billion pairs of feet in the world, the grass is bound to get trampled. When overuse is compounded by automobiles, by ever larger concessions and other forms of exploitation, the wilderness disappears. At Yosemite, one of the oldest wilderness parks, concessionaires backed by politicians almost succeeded in taking over the planning and management of the park. Representatives of Music Corporation of America, whose subsidiary was operating the luxury facilities, upstaged the park rangers and planners, persuading White House officials that businessmen were better able to run a park. This was stopped by citizens who revolted and members of Congress who responded to the complaints. Yet even without the recurring danger of profiteering from the parks at the expense of the public and of nature, the sheer volume of 2½ million visitors a year at Yosemite is overwhelming. When most of the visitors drive instead of walk or take a bus, the result is devastating, painful, and potentially irreversible. The emerging answers are control over the numbers using a given park, having more parks, planning alternative use areas so some spots can have a rest while others are used (as a farmer rotates fields), and sharply curtailing automobile use in wilderness parks (in a nation where thousands walked west, vacationers can perhaps relearn old skills and walk a few miles or share a Park Service Tourmobile). These concerns apply in varying degrees to all major and well-known national parks, not only to Yosemite. The Yellowstone traffic jams are proverbial, compounded by bears—who are trained by tourists to depend on garbage and who line the roadsides—and vacationers willing to risk their children's lives by putting them on a bear's back for a photograph. So even in the wilderness areas set aside, the problem of preserving beauty has become far more convoluted than eliciting the goodwill of nature lovers to step lightly, caressingly on the grass, and to go gently into the good land. No longer even questions of how many go, and where; but how and what happens outside the park, and adjacent to it, that has an impact on the air, the water, and the land and what we build on it.

The Park Service was aware of this national context when Voyageurs was established by Congress in 1970. It was not the first wilderness park to be created from partially used and developed land. Grand Teton had been privately owned and partially developed before becoming a park; so had Virgin Islands and Cape Cod National Seashore and Shenandoah National Park. So had the Sleeping Bear Dunes Lakeshore in Michigan. But Voyageurs presented a unique order of magnitude and complexity, a lake and forest terrain within a larger environmental context. The lessons learned, the successes attained, would become a precedent for future parks, since untouched wilderness to be reserved against onrushing humanity was gone, and new parks would have to be created from partially or wholly developed lands, as Voyageurs had been. The Park Service therefore chose a veteran to get Voyageurs activated.

Myrl Brooks was familiar with the tortuous course of the Voyageurs proposal; now he was assigned the tasks of initiating contact with landowners; translating the plans into trails, facilities, and services to visitors and personnel; and establishing working relationships between Voyageurs and the community around the park and at International Falls, the St. Paul state capitol, and Washington. A burly, ruddy-faced man (his friends say he pretends to be gruff), Brooks has a deep understanding and love of the land, and he had chafed at having to work at desk jobs, which sometimes happens to a successful field man. Outwardly he agreed with Washington co-workers who commiserated with him for being given such a difficult assignment, inwardly he rejoiced. Brooks must be endowed with a bit of acting talent, because when he made his appearance at International Falls in June 1971, he looked and behaved so much the outdoors-type field man that no one felt threatened as they would have been by a manager or bureaucrat; Brooks, working quietly and patiently, is a masterful executive. He had little to work with at first—after a few months a secretary, later two rangers, a very small office. The initial planning, ecological studies, and legal steps were taken (while waiting for the Minnesota lawsuits to run their courses). The association had purchased title to about 30 acres of land within the park, and turned the title over to Brooks, Elmer Andersen making the presentation at ceremonies at Kettle Falls. The association voted to keep up its work, thereby assuring Brooks of an ongoing citizens' organization supporting the park. The Governor's Committee on the park was put in working order, so that state and park interests could mesh. There were meetings and more meetings for a man who would rather be at his sculptures or padding up a Kabetogama Peninsula trail.

Brooks sensed, knew, that the creation of the park would not come about by any dramatic breakthrough, but by steady, often plodding persistence. At times he was subjected to harassment and appeared unruffled, though he must have seethed inwardly. The Park Service was adamant in its opposition to hunting and trapping, and had to be if a healthy ecosystem was to get a start. Yet some political figures in the state and in Washington who knew duck and other hunting could not be done, because Congress and the Park Service had made it a precondition of the park, encouraged local enthusiasts in their efforts to open up the area to hunting (at a time when most of the land had not even been acquired). The effort was bound to fail, and it caused hard feelings and schisms. A wolf carcass was left on the doorstep of the Voyageurs Park Headquarters. A local sportsman, perhaps aiming for elected office, brought publicized suits and challenged Brooks's authority to stop duck hunting, wild-rice harvest, and other incursions. Brooks quietly enforced the law, went through the foreordained court processes.

The impact of snowmobiles on the environment was studied and regulations proposed permitting the use of the open lakes and a few upland trails (to protect snowmobilers from current-weakened ice). It was a compromise seeking to satisfy the snowmobilers while holding environmental impact to a minimum. But someone plowed a winter road over the lake ice, enabling many snowmobiles to enter the area in an open gesture of contempt for the park. In ensuing weeks litter was scattered into the far backreaches of the park, and the first vanguard of winter vacationers, people on cross-country skis and snowshoes, were harassed by snowmobilers who had drunk too much. As with motorcyclists, where the excesses of a few bring ill repute to all, the snowmobile cause received a setback as a consequence. Park planners who had worked hard to please everyone concluded that although snowmobiles did not damage seedling trees as much as had been expected, they interfered with people using the park, which had not been expected, and would impede any effort to reintroduce caribou and elk, or to boost the population of other species.

The important aspects of park planning and creating seemed to be interminably delayed by harassment—frivolous, petty, and fruitless as it seemed to be. That was on the surface. Where it counted, progress was actually rapid; perhaps Brooks and the Park Service even wanted it that way. Purchase of private lands went smoothly, even the massive block of Boise-Cascade lands went into the park quietly. To his surprise, Brooks was contacted by several resort operators who offered to sell their holdings, and their lands and buildings were purchased. Most of the resorts were not winterized and many had been marginal operations. Some elderly owners welcomed the opportunity to retire. In a few instances, arrangements were made for the continued operation of a facility under Park Service supervision, such as the historic Kettle Falls Hotel and concessionaire-operated boat, docking, and lodging at Sullivan Bay, the main entry point to the park off the Ash River Trail. By 1978 nearly 93 percent of the park area was under National Park Service administration.

More Park Service staff were joining Brooks. Rangers, naturalists, and university students were made available in the summer. Youth Conservation Corps participants helped create the first trails and campgrounds, the trails laid out to be nondestination loops enabling hikers and cross-country skiers to sample thoroughly the natural history without feeling the urge to get from one place to another. Park naturalists selected materials for footbridges and trails that would not only blend but would also deteriorate over the years so that another set of trails could be developed, while the old trails were allowed to lapse into their natural state. It was a gentle, careful approach, holding impact to a minimum while seeking to treat people fairly.

The state of Minnesota conducted various studies to complement Brooks's work, one an exhaustive economic and environmental study of the park's periphery. It was probably one of the most thorough and high-quality projects of its kind, but it was not widely read. It analyzed land use and ownership in a broad belt around Voyageurs—climate, soil, demographic, natural, and economic resources, and projected potentials for future use and development. The Park Service obtained the results of several contract studies by archaeologists, foresters, ichthyologists, and other experts, many of them from the University of Minnesota and the Minnesota Historical Society. The studies were essential to knowledgeable management of the park. Lakebottom sediment studies showed that construction of a park headquarters and boat marina, or docking, facilities at Neil Point should be reconsidered; dredging would be required, causing environmental damage to the balance of aquatic life. The experts recommended that the Park Service look at other potential sites, and Black Bay was chosen, where virtually no dredging would have to be done.

Early visitor use showed what before had only been guessed, that the heavier volume would be through Sullivan Bay and the Wooden Frog campground, while traffic to the western end at Black Bay tended to be local people and those on park business. The interpretive centers were being designed accordingly: the center at Sullivan Bay would have more permanent displays, and there would be facilities at the headquarters for rotating displays and art exhibitions.

The budget cycle for a park, or any other government operation, is prolonged and tedious in the extreme. The original park budget was based on the first Master Plan, which had been closely scrutinized by Congress and by the Office of Management and Budget before the legislation was passed. This would serve as a basis for subsequent appropriations and, in part, as a source of the annual plans submitted by personnel at Voyageurs through their regional office in Omaha, and thence to Washington. The annual budget, covering personnel and operating costs as well as construction, maintenance, and repairs, suffers through a three-year cycle. What the Park Service staff needs three years in the future has to be thought out, described, costed, and justified. Usually less money is provided than was requested; rarely it is more. At Voyageurs it has never been more.

Although the three-year budget has to be campaigned through the political labyrinth and faces competition for limited funds at the regional and national levels, the foundation on which it is built changes. The Master Plan is periodically revised. Brooks had to step over the dead wolf on his way to dealing with the future of Voyageurs three, five, ten years hence, and more.

On the periphery of the park other developments could have impact on the delicate work of preserving a regenerating wilderness. Forty-five miles north at Atikokan, Ontario, a new coal-fired power plant is to be built without environmental safeguards against water and air pollution; this could drastically affect water and air in the park. Canada is a foreign country, and the Park Service (from Voyageurs through Omaha to Washington) has to work with the State Department, which has more pressing concerns than a vest-pocket park in northern Minnesota. The assistant secretary of state, who deals with such matters, is probably worried about the Quebec secessionist movement and the renewal of that age-old issue, raised repeatedly on both sides of the border, of whether western Canada should become part of the United States. Jawboning the Canadians into costly pollution controls in one power plant might not be the assistant secretary's foremost concern. Meanwhile at International Falls, Boise Cascade and the Minnesota Environmental Quality officials continue in their prolonged differences about what constitutes adequate and timely compliance with the state's pollution-control regulations. Even nearer at hand, townships control their own zoning; counties are involved in sewage treatment, garbage and trash removal, as well as zoning. These activities, or their absence, affect the park directly and indirectly. For instance, the failure or tardiness of a political unit to cope with a garbage dump can have an impact on the quality of water flowing into the park. A road-construction project immediately outside the park boundaries can pinch off underground water flowage; even logging roads and operations have been known to do this. And not too many miles to the southwest, a new potential danger is in the offing.

Conversion of peat to gas is a new technology, emerging from America's consumptive hunger for energy. America has the second largest peat reserves in the world, after Russia; the bulk of the reserves in the continental U.S. is in Minnesota. A huge pilot plant might be built not far from the park, which could disrupt not only water flow, but also water quality. Peat operations elsewhere have shown that any mechanical disturbance of peat (which is partially decayed organic matter) releases a tremendous number of organic particles, which remain suspended in the water a long time and do not resediment readily. Depending on plant location and operations, a gasification plant could have an impact on park waters, nearby Nett Lake, or Red Lake, where water chemistry and purity are matters of survival. At Nett Lake the economy is heavily dependent on wild rice, at Red Lake on the tribally and cooperatively owned commercial fishing venture. Is there a technology for filtering the particles, perhaps using them to produce a slow-release fertilizer and thereby safeguard the purity of released water? Would developers incur the cost of research and capitalization? Contamination of water is not the only potential hazard in the conversion of peat to gas; air pollution could be an even greater factor.

Less than a hundred miles southeast of the park there is a possibility of copper-nickel mining and smelting just east of the Mesabi Range.

The problems faced by the park's planners and managers shift from year to year as one or another is alleviated or resolved and others appear. No one can predict the inventions and technological changes of the future, nor make provision for them. Which park planner 20 years ago could foresee the advent of snowmobiles? Who could have known 30 years ago that camping vehicles would be manufactured and used extensively?

The Park Service has some unusual resources available; the regional and Washington offices are staffed with biologists, naturalists, landscape architects, planners, engineers, and people in the other disciplines necessary for its operations. Their expertise is available to the field staff. The unusual aspect is the youth and field experience of a significant number of these, and their competence. Some of them are national leaders in their disciplines, consulted not only by Park Service executives but also by the office of the secretary of the interior, by other government departments, and by academicians and scientists outside government. Not a few of these men and women were drawn into public service during the Camelot years of the Kennedy administration.

The head of the planning organization in Washington is both a lawyer and an engineer; although barely 40 years old, he has over a decade of Park Service experience. The leading archaeologist, even younger, has been with the service 15 years and is a national authority on the application of space technology to archaeological research. They and others like them provide vitality as well as skill, reflected and matched by the growing staff at the park headquarters in International Falls.

The Minnesota legislature created a standing commission composed of local residents, legislators, and state officials, known as the Minnesota Citizens Committee on Voyageurs National Park, to work with the Park Service in an advisory and coordinating role and to make recommendations. The head of the Park Service participates in the meetings and works closely with the group. The Voyageurs National Park Association, with its national membership, continues to work on behalf of the park. Nationally there is an influential and prestigious array of park, conservation, and environmental organizations that did not exist 50 years ago, giving voice to changed public values.

All the garnering of human knowledge and energy on behalf of Voyageurs is an expression of the shift in our thinking about what is important. We have decided as a nation that we prefer a healthy environment and the preservation of beauty and places of natural and historic interest to the immediate and short-range gains represented by continued exploitation. Instead of being profligate and spending the capital, represented by natural bounty, we are coming around to a willingness to be content with living on the interest. But if we are to move from the past, with its destruction and damage, to the point where the land and nature (which produced us) can once again nourish us physically and spiritually, a period of transition is required. It is a time when humankind has to act with a certain degree of self-discipline and constraint, to walk lightly on the land and to use it wisely, that it can more readily and sooner share its provender.

The resilience of nature is perhaps one of the greatest miracles. During the fur trade, beavers dwindled to the point where disease all but killed them off, since their numbers had dipped to the minimum point of an adequate gene pool within which healthy specimens can breed. But logging, followed by intense fires, eventually brought a second growth of aspen and birch, and beavers multiplied and spread over the area, the resurgence made possible by the abundance of their principal food. Now some of the "second growth" is beginning to give way to spruce and fir, and the beaver population will probably drop below its present peak numbers in the natural cycle, with the terrain providing sufficient lowlands, aspen, and birch to maintain a lesser but healthy number.

Caribou were eliminated by indiscriminate hunting, including massive slaughter to feed the logging and railroad camps. When logging was followed by intense and repeated fires, even ground and tree lichens, the caribou's principal food, was eliminated. A good forest habitat is returning: the lichens are back and it is now possible to think about restocking the woodland caribou, once the prevalent ungulate. Even elk might be able to return, given a chance, as could wolverine and pine marten.

Reintroduction of woodland caribou may well become a test case of the Park Service's ability to assist the Voyageurs ecosystems to a healthy state. There is sufficient food and terrain; they would fill a place in the animal community being vacated by deer. But will it be possible to bring this about? To obtain the cooperation of snowmobile operators? Of hunters and sportsmen? Perhaps the Canadians and the U.S. Forest Service could enter into a cooperative venture, since all would gain by the return of this natural and necessary member of the wildlife community. Biologists at Voyageurs are convinced that bringing back caribou is the key to a thriving environment. But they also know that it is not a matter of importing one or two animals.

For a species to avoid extinction, there must be a sizable number to form a genetic pool within which healthy specimens can breed. Just what the minimum number is, is being disputed among scientists; but the range is between 100 and 500. Rarities such as the whooping crane are not considered safe from extinction yet because there are too few. The wolves at Yellowstone are considered virtually extinct by naturalists. Too few survive to form a viable genetic pool from which a pack could be formed. This is how one imagines the situation for the few remaining humans scattered here and there after a nuclear holocaust: too few and too damaged to form a genetic pool from which the species could survive.

Whether it can be done with the caribou in Voyageurs Park remains to be seen.

Slowly and gradually, unnecessary buildings within the park are being torn down, the trash accumulations of decades hauled away. Logging roads are growing over, fallen trees blocking the way and wildflowers and plants reasserting themselves. Voyageurs is intended to be a park reached primarily by canoe and boat, and on foot, by ski and snowshoe in the winter. As visitor volume mounts, Park Service tour boats may become available, and motorboats and seaplanes will be confined to channels and areas where their impact will be minimal. Unlike Yosemite, where consideration is being given to reducing traffic by removing paved roads and eliminating some of the luxury facilities, Voyageurs has only two access roads (three if one counts the road to Crane Lake just outside the park) and only modest facilities within the park. Some of these facilities will be retained, the rest removed.

Fluctuating water levels on Kabetogama and Namakan, where the seasonal highs and lows are aggravated by the dam at Kettle Falls, disrupt shorebird nesting, particularly that of loons. Park Service biologists are working with Boise Cascade to diminish the harm done during the nesting season and to ensure that there is enough water in May and June so that the birds will not be stranded. At Lac La Croix where there is no dam the average 4-foot fluctuation permits nesting; on Kabetogama and Namakan it was between 6 and 8 feet before steps were taken to ameliorate it. Brooks believes that more study of water-level fluctuations and their impact on wildlife is needed before one can be certain of the relationships. Border-lakes water levels have always fluctuated wildly, even before the dams were built, and the shorebirds nested and thrived despite low water and floods and seasonal variations. Meanwhile, any protection and stability that can be provided will help. The complexities of the coexistence of humans and a healthy environment are matched only by human complexity itself.

Brooks thinks that we tend to consider environmental impact only in terms of physical effects and that we ignore the reality of what may be the more damaging psychological effects of the machines humans make that intrude on the right to enjoy quiet places that are aesthetically pleasing. Brooks contends that machines disrupt and cause adverse change by their sheer presence, even if they are only quietly rusting back into the earth. At the same time, he recognizes the need for controlled motorized access if the park is to be available to the general public. "It's the usual dilemma of use versus preservation," he says.

Yet it was people, and their changing attitudes, that brought about the conversion of the land into this park. Even the park's proponents changed their views over the course of the years and the events. Andersen who thought the park good for the northland's business, became convinced that conservation and respect for nature were moral, spiritual values. Park opponent Rudy Erickson, International Falls businessman, who thought the federal government was already too big, now belongs to the Voyageurs National Park Association because he wants the park to be the best it can possibly be. Some of George Esslinger's friends who avoided him during the heat of the controversy now walk down the street with him, making remarks about the obvious increase in business at restaurants, motels, and the airport, owing to the presence of the park. Wayne Judy, an early supporter of the park, may at one time have dreamed of International Falls as the snowmobile capital of the world, but he now sees the park as a wilderness treasure to be safeguarded for future generations.

Sportsmen, who long ago pressured the state into not issuing commercial fishing licenses so that there would be more sport fish in Rainy, Namakan, and Kabetogama, have found that conservation is their prime interest, even if the price is the shift to other duck-hunting blinds or supporting the caribou project.

To George Hartzog, head of the Park Service at the time the law establishing it was passed, Voyageurs represented a "filling out of the ecologic fabric. . . . We have to fill the voids we created."

Throughout the new park, in all four seasons, an effort is under way to neutralize the "unnatural influences" of humans, so that today's visiting voyageur, like the voyageurs of the fur trade and the Indian voyageurs before them, can draw nourishment from the land to the enrichment of body and soul.

Majority values in America have shifted toward conservation and a greater regard for the shrinking base of nature: our society does not want to pave it over from coast to coast, and acknowledges a profound need for, and dependence on, nature and natural processes. Yet the dangers continue even after the commitment to these values is made, and one crisis is no sooner surmounted than another appears.

There is a possibility now that an atomic waste dumpground may be established in abandoned mining areas near Atikokan. If this transpires, will there be danger of water seepage from the dump into the border lakes and the park? It is the direction of the flowage. Will there be radiation danger? It is the direction of the prevailing wind.

The national commitment to conservation has been made, but the keeping of the faith is a constant challenge.

10

The Park as Symbol

It is an irony and a paradox of international dimensions. As humanity's needs for the wholesomeness and beauty of the outdoors become more intense, our numbers and economic activities tend to destroy what we seek and require. Can nature, as we think of it and have regarded it over the millennia, continue to survive as a process and an environment in which flora and fauna play out their life chains and interdependencies? As a setting for mankind's participation?

Voyageurs National Park is a test of the proposition that nature can continue to flourish in the presence of one of its own creations, the human species. Perhaps it is not a foregone conclusion that the species, by virtue of its character, introduces a sort of recombinant DNA into the ecological matrix.

The test case of Voyageurs is one of many. We are becoming sensitive to the damage we have done and to its cost. It is an acknowledgment not unique to the United States, but increasingly shared throughout the world. Russians are seeking to save the ecology of Lake Baikal as industry and pollution intrude and destroy; Lake Baikal is also unique and an even more ancient environment than Voyageurs. African countries, although desperately needing foodstuffs and industries, are attempting to safeguard the shrinking fauna and flora at the very heart of humanity's genesis. The problem is universal, the solutions found in one place are of potential use to all. Whatever language we speak and however we conduct our economic affairs, we have come to realize that in choosing between the life processes that produced us and immediate gain, between preservation and exploitation, we deal with values that call for us to decide what is more important for us and within us.

Voyageurs Park is new, the experiment still young. We have this opportunity only because of a campaign conducted by dedicated citizens. There are few countries in the world where it would have been possible for members of society to band together to engage in political activity and citizen diplomacy of the kind and intensity necessary to bring about this park. However, the public concern with nature and the environment is universal, and even in monolithic Russia, where dissent is at personal risk, the citizen outcry influenced the government's decision to try to save the ecological quality of Lake Baikal. Hopefully, the urge to save the earth transcends political systems and divisions.

Minnesota, one small patch of America's north country, has been the setting for a century of pioneering conservation. Publicly supported tree planting took place concurrently with prairie homesteading. The forestry movement had some of its early supporters in Minnesota. The notion of a forest fire-warden system statewide was born here. The very concept of national forests, of applying sustained-yield concepts of timber management to lands in the federal domain, was hammered out in a political compromise over the fate of the lands taken from the Chippewa Indians, giving rise to what ultimately became the Chippewa National Forest as citizens fought for the quality of the land.

The idea of roadless wilderness areas, of lands and waters used exclusively by campers and canoeists, originated here. Slowly, painfully, amid conflict and compromises, the Boundary Waters

Canoe Area approach to public land management developed in the Minnesota north country.

Precedents for national laws and policies expressing our values of how we relate to the land, and how we ought to use it, were pioneered here.

The Indians whose lands were taken and whose lifeways were so forcibly altered were among the earliest to lead the current national renascence of Indian self-determination and self-government. The northern Minnesota reservations at Grand Portage, Nett Lake, Fond du Lac, Leech Lake, Red Lake, White Earth, and Mille Lacs are testing the proposition that Indian culture and sovereignty can survive, can surmount the damage of two centuries, and can flourish. It is an essential ingredient of Indian belief that a wholesome existence stems from respect and the conservation of the land and of the spirit. Western values seem to be moving closer to this belief.

The park traditions that evolved into this western respect of the earth arose from the luxury of old-world aristocrats. In medieval times parks were created by royal grants, perhaps as gestures toward the dispossessed multitudes. Among such parks were formal, manicured gardens, zoos, and a few recreational areas; Schönbrunn and the Prater in Vienna, famous Versailles, Akashi in Japan. It was a romantic concept drifting in the direction of recreation and education, sometimes serving a ritualized role. Islamic parks in which water and cypress trees, symbols of the afterlife, figured importantly, were miniatures of paradise.

Americans moving westward created wilderness parks, setting aside Yellowstone, Yosemite, and others before they could be despoiled and degraded, thereby saving their beauty from the competition for land. Americans also pioneered in the creation of urban parks, such as Central Park in New York City and Rock Creek Park in Washington, D.C. The American traditions and experiences led to early legislation that incorporated recreation, education, and the preservation of wildlife, nature, and historic places. These goals were not always compatible; at times recreational aims clashed with preservation principles.

However imperfect, the American park tradition and the emerging conservation movement have influenced and encouraged similar activities throughout the world. And they are giving us the opportunity to search for answers to a better way of living, to a better safeguarding of nature, that we might better comprehend our own nature.

That we can even test the proposition that nature *can* flourish, that humans are not inherently destructive, proves the issue is still alive, the result not a foregone negative conclusion.

Northern Minnesota, that fecund testground of conservation, and the human imagination have not yet exhausted the possibilities in the search for a more wholesome existence. About 50 years ago some dreamers ventured the notion that the entire area from Lake Superior to Lake of the Woods, on both sides of the border, should be formed into an International Peace Memorial because it was so beautiful, unique, and historic, and because the opportunity for safeguarding or reconstituting the healthy ecosystems still existed. The concept of it was so vast, so seemingly impractical, that it did not come about except by bits and pieces, each of which was considered impossible by some, at one time or another. But the Superior National Forest did come into being, as did the Roadless Area, then the Boundary Waters Canoe Area, then Voyageurs National Park. Perhaps some day an entirely new concept of public land management can be tested here consisting of a combination of zones or areas: forest, park, wilderness, wildlife refuge, industrial, residential, and recreational. Wilder dreams have been tested here and found to be practical.

Meanwhile, Voyageurs National Park is new, and all journeys entail hope and anticipation.

In 1973 Charles Lindbergh returned to Minnesota and spoke at the dedication of a new state park in his hometown of Little Falls, an event sponsored by the Minnesota Historical Society. He said:

> Mankind's achievement is symbolized by the park rather than by satellites and space travel. In establishing parks and nature reserves, man reaches beyond the material values of science and technology. He recognizes the essential value of life itself, of life's natural inheritance irreplaceably evolved through earthly epochs, of the miraculous spiritual awareness

that only nature in balance can maintain. . . . Progress can
be measured only by the quality of life—in all life, not human
life alone. . . . All achievements of mankind have value only
to the extent that they preserve and improve the quality of
life. . . . This is why parks symbolize the greatest advance
our civilization has yet made.

CHRONOLOGY

8000 B.C.– 5000 B.C.	Glacial Lake Agassiz begins to recede, humans probably entering area as uplands emerge
	Prehistoric Indian occupants camp, travel through area; Eastern Archaic Tradition
3000 B.C.	Copper culture
200 B.C.	Laurel Culture, mound building, pottery, continuation of copper working, settlements
700 A.D.– 1500 A.D.	Blackduck Culture, pottery, mounds, settlements, probably ancestors of Sioux
	Ojibway moving east to west on Great Lakes
1494	Cabot at Bay of Fundy, followed by cod-fishing fleets
1500	French ships trade for furs in Bay of St. Lawrence
1536	Cartier at Montreal and Lachine
1608	Quebec founded
1609	Virginia Colony chartered, claims interior (including Minnesota)
1611	Trading post at Montreal
1615	Champlain at Quebec and Lake Huron, probably informed about Lake Superior

1618–20   Brule at Lake Superior

1628–29   Company of One Hundred chartered in Paris:
            Champlain and Richelieu are members

1634   Nicollet at Mackinac and Green Bay, claiming area
            for France

1641   Mission at Sault St. Marie; Montreal grows to a trading
            town; *coureurs de bois* bring back canoe fleets with loads
            of furs

1654   Groseilliers returns with fifty canoes of furs

1659–60   Groseilliers and Radisson on unlicensed trip have furs
            confiscated at Montreal, are arrested, go to London

1660   Fr. Allouez's mission on Madeline Island, mapping of
            Lake Superior and region

1670   Hudson's Bay Company formed in London partly in
            response to presentations by Groseilliers and Radisson,
            and to their book

1671   St. Lusson claims interior of North America for France
            in ceremonies at Sault St. Marie

1673   Joliet on Mississippi via Green Bay, Fox and Wisconsin
            Rivers; mapped, searched for copper in Lake Superior

1678–80   du Lhut (Duluth), lieutenant to Gov. Frontenac,
            winters at Sault St. Marie, at Mille Lacs in spring,
            travels down Mississippi, probably up Minnesota River;
            on trip up Brule and down St. Croix meets three
            emissaries, sent by LaSalle up Mississippi from Illinois,
            who were captured by Sioux and held at Mille Lacs;
            frees them. One of the three is Hennepin, whose later
            books (1683, 1696–97) popularize area.

1683   Duluth establishes forts at St. Croix River,
            Kaministiquia, Nipigon, returns to Mackinac

1688   Duluth challenges Hudson's Bay Company trade

1688–89	deNoyon in Rainy Lake region via Kaministiquia; with Cree
1689	Perrot builds posts on Wisconsin side of upper Mississippi
1690	French explore Grand Portage and Minnesota River routes west
1692	French convoke meeting of traders and *coureurs de bois* from interior; 200 attend on August 17
	LeSueur at Madeline post
1694–95	LeSueur at post on island at mouth of St. Croix, applies for upper Mississippi monopoly
1700–1701	LeSueur up Mississippi from mouth to Minnesota River, establishes Ft. L'Huillier at Blue Earth on Minnesota River
1713	British regain Hudson's Bay by Treaty of Utrecht
1717	deNoyon builds post on Rainy Lake
1727	Verendrye stationed at Nipigon, has map drawn by Auchagah showing route to salt water
1731	Verendrye winters at Kaministiquia, one son and a nephew are at Rainy Lake where Ft. St. Pierre is erected, becomes permanent trading post
1732	Verendrye pushes inland, builds post on Lake of the Woods at Northwest Angle (Ft. St. Charles), plants vegetable gardens
1733	Verendrye's nephew Jeremaye takes furs back to Montreal, returns by August
1735	Approximate date of Ojibway occupancy of Rainy Lake area, hitherto occupied by Cree, Monsoni, Assiniboin, and traversed by Sioux; Cree allied to Ojibway, move northwest; Sioux and Ojibway warfare intensifies

1736	Sioux kill 21 of Verendrye's men, including one of his sons, on Lake of the Woods island; Bourassa trading post built on Vermilion River detroit at Crane Lake; Battle of Cutfoot Sioux between Ojibway and Sioux
1738	Verendrye expedition to Mandan country, Missouri, possibly to Rockies
1740	Battle of Kathio: Ojibway drive Sioux from Mille Lacs
1740–50	Bitter rivalry between Verendrye's son Joseph and trader Marin (conflict between Grand Portage vs. Fox River)
1742–43	Verendrye posts built at Winnipeg, on Assiniboine and Saskatchewan Rivers
1763	British take over Canada from French
1764	British call conference of Ojibway at Niagara
1765	British trader robbed at Rainy Lake by goods-starved Indians; similar incident in 1767, posts nevertheless built throughout area
	Alexander Henry, trader, at Sault St. Marie and Chequamaugon, searches for ore; Henry had escaped when Ojibway attacked and killed British garrison at Mackinac in1763 toward end of British-French war
1767	Carver at Grand Portage
1768	Grand Portage fort constructed by John Askin; annual rendezvous probably began earlier
1771	Battle of St. Croix Falls between Ojibway and alliance of Sioux, Sac and Fox
1774	Northeast Minnesota part of Quebec Province
1778	Jonathan Carver's book excites interest in area
1779	North West Company formed by amalgamation of several partnerships; the company's governors attend annual rendezvous at Grand Portage, as do Montreal

merchants; annual trade of 40,000 pounds sterling, involving over 500 people and 12 soldiers

1780 (ca.)   Peter Pond travels to Athabasca, Great Slave Lake; gross business in 1780 reaches $20,000

1783   John Tanner, age 10, captured across from Miami River mouth in Kentucky, was adopted and raised by Ojibway; his narrative is a prime information source for 1780–1820 life in the region

By treaty Britain gives up border-lakes area to United States but retains control

1787   Northwest Territory established by United States; Northwest Ordinance

1789   Alexander Mackenzie travels border route to Mackenzie River

1792–93   Mackenzie to Peace River, across Rockies to Pacific

1793   Hudson's Bay builds post at Rainy Lake outlet; forced out by North West in 1798

1797   Cartographer David Thompson, employed by North West, maps Lake of the Woods, Dakotas, Mandans, 49th Parallel, back via Mississippi headwaters area, Red Lake, Duluth, Sault St. Marie, and Grand Portage in ten months

X Y Company, rivaling North West, formed at Grand Portage

1800   Northeast Minnesota part of Indiana Territory, on paper

1804   X Y joins North West, both abandon Grand Portage and move to Ft. William to avoid possible American control and customs

1806   Lt. Zebulon Pike of the U.S. Army raises American flag over northeast Minnesota

1808   John Jacob Astor founds American Fur Company

1809	Northeast Minnesota in Illinois Territory, on paper
1812	Hudson's Bay and North West cut back operations on American side
	Indian prophet urges revolt against whites, unrest in area
	Selkirk establishes Red River settlement
1816	Hudson's Bay, directed by Selkirk, sends Swiss mercenaries to recapture Rainy Lake post
	Congress passes law prohibiting foreigners from engaging in fur trade on American side, probably urged by Astor
1818	Hudson's Bay rebuilds Rainy Lake post; northeast Minnesota in Michigan Territory, on paper
1821	North West Company and Hudson's Bay amalgamate
1822	First U.S. Indian Agency at Sault St. Marie; British and American boundary commissioners explore area
1823	American Fur Company establishes post on Rainy Lake opposite Hudson's Bay
1825–26	Prairie du Chien and Fond du Lac Indian treaties
1833	American Fur Company and Hudson's Bay agree to eliminate competition, AFC moves west
1836	Northeast Minnesota becomes part of Wisconsin Territory
1837	Ojibway Treaty, first annuities
1840	Beginning of commercial fishing on Lake Superior
1842	Webster-Ashburton Treaty sets U.S.-Canada boundary
	Financial panic, American Fur Company fails, ends operations in 1847 owing to bitter trade wars, chaotic conditions

1848	Wisconsin becomes a state, leaving Minnesota without government for a few months; Minnesota Territory formed 1849
1849	Owen geological survey of northeast Minnesota
1854	Major treaty with Ojibway, land cessions
1855	Treaty with Pillagers, land cessions
1857	Dawson-Hinds survey leading to Dawson Trail
1858	Minnesota becomes a state
1863	Treaty establishing Leech Lake Reservation; also treaties at Red Lake/Pembina
1864	Ojibway treaties
1865	Lake Vermilion gold rush
1866	Bois Fort treaty
1869–70	First Riel rebellion; Wolseley troops hack Dawson Trail
1884	First iron ore shipped from Vermilion Range
1884–85	Second Riel rebellion; Riel captured and executed
1890	Iron discovered on Mesabi Range; extensive logging by large companies
1891	Minnesota legislature proposes a national park for border lakes
1893	Gold discovered in Rainy Lake area; Rainy Lake City built
1894	Koochiching plat surveyed and filed
1901	Village of Koochiching incorporated
1903	Koochiching changes name to International Falls
1905	Work begun on construction of dam at Koochiching Falls

1907   First railroad trains arrive at International Falls

1908   Minnesota (Chippewa) National Forest established by Congress

1909   Superior National Forest established; United States and Canada establish International Joint Commission

1910   Paper mill at International Falls begins operations

1912   Lake of the Woods Reference sent to International Joint Commission

1916   Insulite mill begins production

1917   IJC issues opinion on Lake of the Woods Reference

1925   Rainy Lake Reference comes before IJC

1926   BWCA Roadless Area

1930   Shipstead-Nolan Act

1934   IJC issues opinion on Rainy Lake Reference

1938   Joint Minnesota–Park Service survey of state park and recreation plans cites Kabetogama Peninsula as potential park site

1948   Thye-Blatnik Act; M & O Paper Company considers offering its Kabetogama Peninsula holdings to Minnesota in exchange for state-held lands

1949   President Truman bans planes from BWCA

1957   Minnesota renews exploration of national park status for Kabetogama Peninsula area

1960   Multiple Use Act

National Park Survey updates 1938 study, finds Kabetogama site a good potential for national park status

1962   Minnesota Gov. Elmer Andersen renews park proposal; the name Voyageurs National Park is coined by Sigurd Olson on tour of area by state and national officials

1962–63	National Park Service field-study teams visit Kabetogama area
1964	Wilderness Act
	National Park Service recommends establishment of Voyageurs National Park
1965	Minnesota Outdoor Recreation Resources Commission holds public hearings on park, issues report; M & O purchased by Boise Cascade Corporation; Voyageurs National Park Association established; 5,000 citizens sign petition for park at Minnesota state fair
1966	Interior Secretary's Advisory Board on National Parks recommends establishment of Voyageurs
1967	Minnesota Outdoor Recreation Resources Commission reaffirms call for Voyageurs; National Park Service also reaffirms choice of Voyageurs as "the outstanding remaining opportunity . . . in the northern lake country."
	Citizens Committee for Voyageurs National Park chaired by Dr. Mayo joins VNPA in campaigning for park; state-sponsored conference on pros and cons of park held; governor calls for park to include Crane Lake area
1968	Park legislation introduced by Blatnik and Mondale; Izaak Walton League supports
1969	Park legislation reintroduced by Blatnik and Mondale; hearings held at International Falls; Fish and Wildlife assessment of area; Charles Lindbergh tours area, endorses Voyageurs proposal
1970	Hearings on park legislation held in Washington, D.C.; House and Senate pass Voyageurs Park bill
1971	President Nixon signs Voyageurs National Park bill; Minnesota begins process to transfer title of state lands to Park Service; Park Service opens office in International Falls

1974   Transfer of state lands to Park Service

1975   Voyageurs National Park formally established

1973–80   Master plan developed; final approval in 1980

1980–98   Wilderness designation of Kabetogama Peninsula, recommended after hearings, pending. Study and recommendation required by original legislation but decision by Secretary of Interior still not made, probably due to political pressure. Citizens Council opposed designation, VRNPA brought suit in 1992 to effectuate.

1983   Park boundaries revised, portion of Black Bay area removed from park to accommodate local sportsmen

1988   Visitor centers and trails opened, Kettle Falls Hotel renovated

1995–96   Three congressional hearings (one in Washington) on greater motorized use of Voyageurs Park and BWCAW, at behest of newly elected Sen. Rod Grams (R., Minn.)

1996–97   Hearings by U.S. Park Service; U.S. Mediation on park and BWCAW issues in dispute, such as motorized access and use

SUGGESTED READING

Backes, David. 1997. *A Wilderness Within: The Life of Sigurd F. Olson.* Minneapolis: University of Minnesota Press.

Bolz, J. Arnold. 1960. *Portage into the Past: By Canoe along the Minnesota-Ontario Boundary Waters.* Minneapolis: University of Minnesota Press.

Hazard, Evan B. 1982. *The Mammals of Minnesota.* Minneapolis: University of Minnesota Press.

Heinselman, Miron. 1996. *The Boundary Waters Wilderness Ecosystem.* Minneapolis: University of Minnesota Press.

Jaques, Florence Page. 1938. *Canoe Country.* Minneapolis: University of Minnesota Press.

———. 1944. *Snowshoe Country.* Minneapolis: University of Minnesota Press.

Nute, Grace Lee. 1941. *The Voyageur's Highway: Minnesota's Border Lake Land.* St. Paul: Minnesota Historical Society Press.

———. 1950. *Rainy River Country: A Brief History of the Region Bordering Minnesota and Ontario.* St. Paul: Minnesota Historical Society Press.

Olson, Sigurd F. [1956] 1997. *The Singing Wilderness.* Reprint, Minneapolis: University of Minnesota Press.

———. [1958] 1997. *Listening Point.* Reprint, Minneapolis: University of Minnesota Press.

Searle, R. Newell. 1977. *Saving Quetico-Superior: A Land Set Apart.* St. Paul: Minnesota Historical Society Press.

United States National Park Service. 1980. *Voyageurs National Park Master Plan.* Washington, D.C. : Government Printing Office.

———. 1983. *Wilderness Recommendation, Voyageurs National Park.* Denver: U.S. Department of the Interior, National Park Service.

Warren, William. [1885] 1984. *History of the Ojibway People.* St. Paul: Minnesota Historical Society Press.

INDEX

177

ROBERT TREUER is a writer and a tree farmer near Bemidji, Minnesota. His published books are *The Tree Farm: Replanting a Life* and *A Northwoods Window*. His short stories and articles have appeared in the *Atlantic, Yankee, Washingtonian,* and other periodicals. He has written hundreds of newspaper essays, many widely syndicated or reprinted.